What Readers
Modern Management Made Easy Books

"The lessons I learned reading *Modern Management Made Easy* books make me a better leader. Descriptive examples paint a clear picture of situations at work I often find myself in, and applying the practical advice helps me better serve myself, my team, and my organization. Johanna influenced me to think congruently, and provided the tools needed to excel in my role. I can't recommend these books highly enough."

— Carl Hume, VP Engineering at HomeStars

"If you are starting a new management role, or simply want a reminder of what it is all about, then these books provide a body of practical wisdom in an easily digestible form. They place the role of the manager in a wider context rather that implying some context free set of qualities and manage to avoid the platitudes all too common in books of this kind."

—Dave Snowden, Chief Scientific Officer, Cognitive Edge

"Do you need real-world answers to real-world management problems, especially to address agility at all levels? As I read Johanna Rothman's *Modern Management Made Easy* books, I nodded along and said, "I've seen that!" Use these books with their suggestions for what you can do to solve your real-world management problems."

— Scott Seivwright, Agile Coach and Leadership Pirate

"This series of books is a rare mix of personal stories, practical examples, researched theory, and direct calls-to-action. Rarer still, Johanna's writing segues between them without losing the reader or breaking their immersion. Whether you are a manager, an aspiring manager, or a coach of managers, these books will give you the necessary tools to develop new skills and the language to develop new cultures."

— Evan Leybourn, Co-Founder, Business Agility Institute

"Think of these books like three friends who can offer you advice on your management journey. You'll return to them whenever you want advice, reassurance, challenge, or renewal. I added these books to my library, right next to the late Russell Ackoff's books on the F/laws of management. Use these books to create your modern management and an environment that brings out the best in the people you lead and serve."

—Claude Emond, Organizational Performance-Growth Expert

"This book series is the furthest thing from your run-of-the-mill boring management books. Johanna Rothman busts dozens of management myths in an easy to read set of essays that are useful in part or as a whole. The stories and anecdotes told are relatable, practical, and fit for today's modern workplace. Regardless of your management experience, there's valuable lessons to be found on every single page."

—Ryan Dorrell, Co-Founder, AgileThought

"These books provide a wealth of practical leadership and team-building information. Project managers and leaders of problem-solving teams are often taught logical but flawed guidance from the industrial era. Today's project teams require servant leadership, inspiration, and collaboration skills far more than centralized planning or progress tracking. Johanna's books identify and bring to life better alternatives for undertaking challenging projects. Laid out in a helpful sequence, they provide a wealth of practical tools for today's practitioner searching for better outcomes and more satisfied stakeholders."

—Mike Griffiths, CEO, Leading Answers Inc.

"If you lead at any level in today's disrupted and crazy world, read these books on modern management. As with all Johanna's books, they are full of insightful stories, real world examples and concrete actionable advice. Use these books to guide your own development, support and lead others, and guide your organisation to greater success."

—Shane Hastie, Director of Community Development ICAgile

"Each product team has its own culture. It is important for leaders to understand where culture comes from and how they can influence it so that their teams can build better products. In the *Modern Management Made Easy* books, Johanna Rothman has some valuable advice to help you be more purposefully create a culture that will support the team while driving powerful innovations. Her style of writing includes questioning and addressing industry myths that draw from decades of real world experience. Her work will change the way you lead product."

—Sean Flaherty, EVP of Innovation and cohost of the Product Momentum podcast.

"With her characteristic blend of pragmatism, insight, and wit, Johanna Rothman takes on the role of modern management's mirror, mythbuster, and mentor. The first in her *Modern Management Made Easy* trilogy, *Practical Ways to Manage Yourself* demystifies the illusions we knowledge workers spin. Offering thought-provoking observations from her own career, along with steps to help identify and replace outmoded thinking and habits while gently urging guiding the reader towards a more thoughtful management practice, this latest volume reinforces why Johanna remains among modern management's most readable, relevant, and respected thinkers."

—Tonianne DeMaria, Coauthor of Shingo-award winning *Personal Kanban*

"With two decades of management experience, I found myself nodding at every question and recognizing every myth. If you always work the way you've always seen management, you might not realize your alternatives. Do yourself a favor, and read these books because people won't complain to you—they'll complain about you."

—Mun-Wai Chung, Senior Consultant, MunWai Consulting

"I've had a few good managers and mentors to emulate in my management and consulting journey. But I sure could have used these three books along the way. There are many pragmatic gems here I wished I had back then, and there are still more gems that I now know I'll be using moving forward."

—JF Unson, Agility Coach/Catalyst

"If you've ever wondered about management and why things are the way they are, read these books. Johanna offers questions—questions I hear every day—and then possibilities for improvement. Her personal and client stories challenged my thinking, for the better. Even if you only read the sections about managing performance, these books will help you select actions that create engagement and better performance in your organization."

—John Cutler, Head Customer Education, Amplitude

Practical Ways to Manage Yourself

Modern Management Made Easy: Book 1

Johanna Rothman

Practical Ink
Arlington, Massachusetts

Practical Ways to Lead and Serve (Manage) Others

Modern Management Made Easy: Book 1

Johanna Rothman

Published by Practical Ink
www.jrothman.com

Cover design: Brandon Swann, swanndesignstudio.com
Cover art: Company Value Icons by Angela Cini, on depositphotos.com

Ebook: 978-1-943487-12-7
Print: 978-1-943487-13-4
Hardcover: 978-1-943487-14-1

In memory and honor of Jerry Weinberg who told me I should write a book about rewiring management logic.

For Edward Rothman, my first management mentor.

And, for Mark, Shaina and Adam, and Naomi and Matt, as always. Thank you for managing me.

Contents

List of Figures

Acknowledgments

I thank all the people who read and commented on the management myths columns as I wrote them. I also thank Software Quality Engineering, now known as Techwell, who first published these columns.

I thank my coaching and consulting clients. You have taught me more than you know.

I thank Matt Barcomb, Pawel Brodzinski, Lisa Crispin, Andrea Goulet, Mike Lowery, Carl Hume, and Leland Newsom for their technical review.

I thank Rebecca Airmet and Nancy Groth for their editing. I thank Brandon Swann for his cover design. I thank Karen Billipp for her layout and Jean Jesensky for her indexing.

Any mistakes are mine.

Introduction

Several years ago, I wrote a series of articles I called "management myths." They each described one way I'd seen managers act so that the manager created the opposite result from the one they wanted. Yes, the manager's actions created precisely the opposite effect.

I wrote a myth a month for 36 months.

I assumed as the world transitioned to agile approaches or approaches where teams, managers, and organizations needed more resilience, that managers would change. I thought no one needed to read about the myths in a world where we want collaborative, cross-functional self-managing teams.

I was wrong.

As I worked with more managers who wanted to use agile approaches, I saw several problems with their management practices:

- The practices barely worked for non-agile teams. Teams succeeded in spite of their management.
- The practices prevented any team's adaptability and resilience.
- The practices didn't work for managers who wanted to lead and serve others.

And, in an organization attempting to transform to an agile culture? The more the managers tried to make old patterns work, the less agility anyone exhibited.

Why did these smart people behave in ways that didn't make sense?

They didn't know any better.

These managers had never witnessed useful management, never mind excellent management. They tried to do the best job they could. And, they perpetuated what they'd experienced, or possibly even learned in school. They practiced what they'd seen—the old ways of management.

It's time for real modern management.

Modern managers face enormous challenges. Too many managers feel as if they are stuck between the proverbial rock and a hard place.

How can you become a modern manager when the system, the culture, is based on old thinking and old practices?

Carefully.

I've divided the original essays into three books. The first—this one—asks you to consider how you can manage and respect yourself to build congruence and integrity in your actions.

Book 2, *Practical Ways to Lead and Serve (Manage) Others*, explains how you can serve a harmonic whole. The entire team or group can then work together in a culture of transparency and trust.

Book 3, *Practical Ways to Lead an Innovative Organization*, explores ways to create a human and innovative culture in your organization, so you can use the ideas of trust and integrity to create a place where people want to work.

You might feel many constraints in your situation. As you read these books, you might nod and say, "Yes, I can do that." And, you might shake your head at some ideas and say, "Not going to touch that here. Nope, not at all."

I do hope you consider each essay as a possible experiment for your management practice. You have options.

Who Are the People in These Essays?

You might wonder about my use of names and gender in these books. For example, you might never have seen women as senior managers. I have seen men and women as senior managers. I've been a senior manager.

My experience tells me that a given gender does not equate to great or unfortunate management skills. Neither does a person's country of origin or any other kind of individual demographic.

To help you see what the management world could be, I've created parity across genders. I've used names of people I've worked with or admired. Even with that, I've changed all the names to protect the innocent and the guilty.

I've had the good fortune to meet and work with male and female managers worldwide. In almost every circumstance, the managers have done the best they could, given their company's environment and culture. The manager's gender didn't matter.

The company's environment mattered more than anything. You might—or might not—see the variety of people in roles that I write about here.

Through my work, I've recognized several principles that create great management and build healthy organizational cultures.

1. Clarify purpose—for you, the team, and the organization.
2. Build empathy with the people who do the work.
3. Build a safe environment. People work better when they can trust you, their colleagues, and the organization as a whole.
4. Seek outcomes by optimizing for an overarching goal.
5. Encourage experiments and learning.

6. Catch people succeeding.
7. Exercise value-based integrity as a model for the people you lead and serve.

All three books build on these principles:

- Respect—for yourself, for the team, and for the purpose of the organization.
- Trust—possibly with boundaries—to encourage the behaviors and outcomes you want.
- Team-based approaches to working at all levels of the organization.

All three books explain some of the trickier parts of management. You'll get the most value if you read all three books.

As you read the dialogue in the essays, remember that I said most of these things to my managers. You might see these conversations as insubordination.

I didn't feel as if I was insubordinate. I used the principle of congruence to have conversations where my manager and I cared about the outcome, each other, and discovered our best possible outcome for the situation.

You and I are different people. How I frame conversations might not work for you. You will find *your* best ways to describe the situation and influence your manager.

You can practice human and humane management that produces superior results for your organization. You can respect yourself, the people you serve, and the entire organization as well as customers. You can act with integrity. And, you can have empathy without being a pushover.

Management is an honorable profession. We need managers—great, congruent managers who can use their interpersonal skills to get the best out of themselves first. Then, they can extend those skills to the people they serve and across the organization.

My best to you. I hope you enjoy reading these essays and that you ease your way into modern management.

Let's start.

CHAPTER 1

Management Starts with Managing Yourself

Great management starts with managing yourself.

You might share several commonly held beliefs: that management starts with managing others. Or, that management starts with organizational design so other people can accomplish the work.

Great management includes those two parts. However, the way we, as managers, manage our work, our beliefs, and our actions around other people is the best predictor of great management.

Our assumptions and experience color our approach to management. Especially if you've never seen great management.

Great managers work to serve, not control. They make sure they create trusting relationships with others. They do that by delegating, coaching, and creating an environment where everyone can contribute.

Great managers manage themselves to serve others.

The reality is that too many managers feel pressure to deliver or "perform." Too many managers interpret that pressure as:

- As the expert, they can't delegate the work; they must do the work.
- They can't trust others to do the work correctly; they must micromanage the work to make sure the work is done right.
- They can't admit they don't know something.
- They can't admit any mistake because then no one would believe they know what to do or how to do it.

Management is not easy. Ever. But managing like that makes your job much more difficult than it needs to be.

When you try to meet those pressures to "perform," your actions disconnect the people you lead from the work. You might interpret that disconnection as a "lack of engagement" on the part of the people you serve.

Here are some indications your management actions might not work for you:

- You think of management as "herding cats," even though you see humans in the office every day.
- When you try to help, you make the situation worse.
- You wonder why people react negatively to you when you try to do your job or offer help.

I've had helpful managers and disastrous managers. They all *thought* they were doing a good job.

Helpful managers facilitate everyone's work through various leadership approaches. These managers create and refine the organizational culture in which people can deliver their best work and thrive. When managers balance the needs of the people inside the organization with the needs of the customers to achieve business outcomes, everyone wins.

I love helpful management.

And, there are other kinds of managers. These people tend to micromanage. They tend to do the work themselves instead of teaching others. They make decisions when they have no data and they dither when they have data.

Worse, these not-so-helpful managers often insert themselves into the work. They either insist on doing the work, or they create control points where people need to tell the manager what they're doing. Way too often.

These not-so-helpful managers rarely admit when they make mistakes. They might be afraid to admit they aren't the smartest person in the room. Or, they think admitting a mistake is a sign of weakness. Or, they attempt to ignore the problem and continue with no acknowledgment they created a problem. Worse yet, they are genuinely unaware that there is a problem.

When we manage ourselves, we help people grow and learn. We explain the purpose of the work and the constraints around the work. We delegate. We coach. We build trust so we can clarify the direction and then trust people to do a great job.

Managers who manage themselves don't insert themselves into the work. They have the managerial capacity to remove impediments and serve the people they lead.

Managers who manage themselves exhibit congruence, more often than not.

1.1 Discover Your Management Balance with Congruence

You have a tough job as a manager. Your managers might pressure you to "do more with less." You might be going through an agile transformation and wondering what your job really is. You might have to hire—or worse—lay off or fire people to manage to the organization's demand or revenue. You might have other issues that challenge you in your role as a manager.

How do you balance all these competing pressures? Consider congruence, as described in *Software Quality Management, Vol 2: First-Order Measurement* [WEI93]. I have found the idea of congruence helpful as a frame for my management thinking.

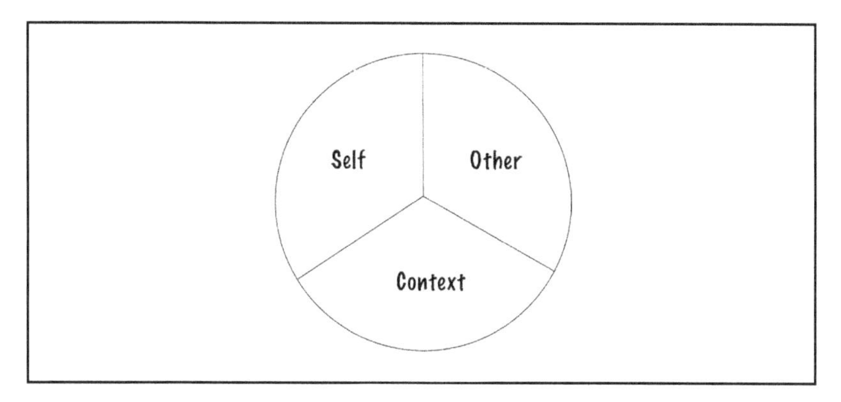

Figure 1.1: Congruence

Congruence is a way to find your balance between you and your needs, the other person and their needs, and the entire context.

If you ignore the needs of the other person, you might blame people. One senior manager once said to me, "Those testers. They keep finding problems. We can't ship when I want to." The senior manager blamed the testers for doing their job. Notice that he didn't blame the developers, the people who—due to pressure from him—had created the problems.

If you ignore yourself and your needs, you might placate or appease other people. One senior manager said, "I always say yes to any requests from my peers. I must accommodate their needs." When I asked him about the costs in terms of burnout, he said, "It's up to us to make sure the organization succeeds." His department had the highest turnover in the entire organization.

If you ignore the people in the situation, you might be super-reasonable, thinking you can apply *only* reason to the situation. One team had suffered a tragedy—their technical leader had died suddenly from fast-moving cancer. Six months later, the team still had not recovered. In fact, they left "his" chair vacant in their meetings. When I asked their manager what he had done to help the team move through their grief, the manager said, "I've thought about it. The team should have finished grieving by now."

If you ignore all three: yourself, the others, and the context, you act in irrelevant ways. One senior manager hated conflict. Some people on his management team excelled at arguing loudly. Just when his management team would get to the meat of the argument, he would start to talk about the weather. Or his favorite sports team. Anything other than the issue at hand. He acted in an irrelevant way.

These managers weren't inherently stupid, bad, or wrong. They were incongruent. And, they didn't realize the effect their words and actions had on the people they served.

If you don't think about the whole—self, other, and context—you have a lopsided view of the system. In management, if you don't think about yourself, the other people, and the environment, you have a lopsided view of everything: the people you serve, their teams or group, and the organization as a whole.

You might blame others if you stop thinking about them as humans. (A quick check: do you talk about resources instead of people?) You might placate others if you stop thinking about yourself—you appease or accommodate others at a cost to you or the people you serve. You might consider actions that make life more difficult for all the people if you don't think about the context, the entire organizational system. If you don't want to deal with any of the people or the context, you might act in an irrelevant way.

I often think of management as trying to stay balanced on a multi-sided balance beam. Lean too far one way, the people lose respect for you and their peers. Lean too far another way and your management thinks you can't do your job. Lean too far the third way and you don't do right by the customers or the organization.

Where to Start with Congruence?

Consider starting with yourself when you think about congruence. When I ask myself if I'm blaming or placating or being super-reasonable or irrelevant, I find it easier to see my balance or my lack of balance.

Managers have a lot to consider to discover and maintain their emotional and management balance.

In my experience, the worst managers show their incongruence when they implode in some way. In *The No Asshole Rule: Building a Civilized Workplace and Surviving One That Isn't* [SUT07], Bob Sutton has an entire chapter on the damage bad managers do and the consequences to the people they manage, their products and organizations, and their reputations. Being a jerk has grave consequences.

1.2 Manage With Value-Based Integrity

Managers who are congruent put their integrity first. When I think of integrity, I think of how we live our values and how those values create a resilient, integrated whole approach to congruent management.

I look for people who live these values:

- Honesty, which means explaining what you want and admitting when you're wrong.
- Fairness, which means balancing the needs of everyone.
- Consistency, which means others can predict your behaviors within some bounds.
- Truthfulness, which means helping everyone understand the true state of the situation.
- Respect for others, which means creating an environment in which people can do their best work, trusting people to do a great job, and not gossiping about others.

Congruent Values Create Integrity

I've met some managers who thought it was fine to lie to other people. Lying was part of their value system. While they were congruent with themselves and their personal values, they were not congruent with the greater context or the organization.

When an entire organization fails to live these values of honesty, fairness, consistency, responsibility, and respect, the entire organization can fail. Enron, as an example, went bankrupt. The CEO of Wells Fargo was forced to resign.

You might think of other possibilities for integrity. When I start with congruence, I'm more than part way there.

1.3 Self-Esteem Builds Empathy and Respect for Yourself

When you think of empathy and respect, you may first think of other people. That is part of management, and I discuss it in depth in the second book in this series.

For now, consider how you might need to feel empathy and respect for yourself. Do your managers ever ask you to do anything that violates your integrity? If so, and you placate your managers, then you start to lose your self-respect. You might lose empathy with yourself.

You certainly lose your self-esteem.

What's the worst thing that could happen if you say no to those requests?

I was a Director of Software Quality at one unnamed organization years ago. The senior managers asked me to "certify" a release. My role was to "certify" that we had no major problems in the release.

I managed not to laugh out loud when they asked me, because we had *just* finished a meeting where I'd explained about the problems I knew about and the effects of those problems. I asked this question, "What do you want to happen?"

The CEO said, "I want to be able to ship so we gain revenue."

I said, "Okay, we can remove these features." I listed them. "And, we can go back to last month's codebase because the performance was better."

He shook his head. "Not good enough. The Very Important Customer (VIC) is paying for this because of the features on that list."

"Want me to explain what's going on with the software? I can call and explain. VIC and I have built trust."

"No, I want you to certify the release," he said.

"But, I'll break the trust I've built," I said.

"Too bad."

I said no, and left. I walked back to my office and called my husband to explain I might not have a job later that day. That would have been a problem for us because I carried our health insurance.

Was I nervous? Of course.

Did I regret anything? No, absolutely not. My personal integrity was at stake.

When we exercise our personal integrity, it's true, we might lose our job or a specific role. However, even *I* have never immediately lost a job. Very few managers lose their jobs if they say, "No," to a management request that lacks integrity. The people who make those requests *know* the requests are wrong.

This CEO wasn't stupid or bad. He was trying to get a short-term gain for the long-term survival of the company. I am sure he felt as if he was between the proverbial rock and a hard place.

I had enough self-esteem to manage my integrity and congruence. I was able to maintain my integrity. If I'd been a single parent, would I have made a different choice? I'd like to think not, but that wasn't my situation.

Self-esteem drives our congruence, integrity, and empathy. I'm not talking about fake "pumping ourselves up" but about realizing our strengths and weaknesses and managing them. The more self-esteem we have, the more we are able to manage ourselves.

When I have self-esteem, I see how to take myself out of the middle of the work. That means I coach and delegate so other people can practice doing the work instead of—or maybe even better than—doing it myself.

You might like some of the books on this reading list. They can help you explore your self-esteem and how vulnerable you might feel at times:

- Weinberg's *More Secrets of Consulting: The Consultant's Toolkit* [WEI02]. Don't worry about the title. Everyone needs to understand their self-esteem toolkit. Every manager needs to learn, at the very least, how to say no. This book may help you learn to do so.

- Brown's *Daring Greatly: How the Courage to Be Vulnerable Transforms the Way We Live, Love, Parent, and Lead* [BRO12]. Much of modern management is having the courage to work differently.
- Brown's *The Gifts of Imperfection: Let Go of Who You Think You're Supposed to Be and Embrace Who You Are* [BRO10]. When I realized I couldn't be perfect at all things, I could choose how to exploit my strengths and manage my imperfections. I became a much better manager.

When we are congruent, we can be authentic. That authenticity arises from our self-esteem.

When we are congruent and have self-esteem, we can move ourselves from doing the work to facilitating the work. That's why managers coach and delegate.

1.4 Managers Serve and Lead Others

You may have heard the term, "servant leadership." Robert Greenleaf coined the term in his classic, *Servant Leadership: A Journey into the Nature of Legitimate Power and Greatness* [GRE02].

In *The Case for Servant Leadership* [KEI08], Kent Keith defines seven practices of servant leaders:

1. They are self-aware.
2. They listen.
3. They serve the people who work "for" them.
4. They help other people grow.
5. They coach people, not control them.
6. They unleash the energy and intelligence of others.
7. They work to develop their foresight, so they can act instead of react.

When managers act as servant leaders, they enable and encourage the people they serve to do the best job possible. (Keith calls this "Changing the Pyramid.")

I worry when I hear phrases like these:

- "My" people
- "I own" this department
- "My people know they are accountable" for some task or deliverable.

Managers don't "own" people or departments. People can account for their work for a given task or deliverable. However, accountability does not mean the people know about or can deliver that task or deliverable. (There's a great discussion about responsibility and accountability in *The Responsibility Process* [AVE16].)

These ownership and accountability words pervade management in our organizations. However, those words do not explain what managers do.

Managers lead the organization in many ways. Book 3 has much more about organizational leadership. Managers serve others. Book 2 has much more about how to serve others.

One way to lead and serve is to manage the system.

1.5 Managers Manage the System

When I first became a manager, I had to learn how to remove myself from the day-to-day work so I could focus on the team as a whole. I didn't manage the work. I managed the system, so everyone could do a great job.

Managers manage the system so everyone can contribute.

I discovered I needed to help the system of work in these areas:

- The bottlenecks in the team. Sometimes, people need tools. Sometimes, people need feedback or to learn something specific. Depending on what people need, I might offer feedback or help someone else offer that feedback. I might coach or ask who else would be a better coach. I might train or offer specific training.

- Information people needed to make good decisions. I often discovered I was the bottleneck for their decisions. I learned how to delegate.
- The time people spent either stuck on a problem or pursuing dead-end solutions. Too often, people were reluctant to say they were wrong or stuck—especially in public. I made it possible for people to admit they were wrong or stuck and to fix a problem fast because I modeled that behavior.

As a manager, you need to know enough about the work so you can ease the way to a better environment. Your job is *not* to jump in and do the work for them. They can't learn if you do the work. And, you can't be an effective manager if you do a lot of technical work.

What does knowing enough about the work mean? You need to know enough to see when people are stuck. You need to know the dynamics of the work. You can see bottlenecks, even if your team or group can't. You can see if anyone needs more training even if they might not know. Your job is to take a longer-term perspective to see if the team or group needs tools or different metrics, or where a different approach might help.

Your job is not to impose or inflict help on a person, team, or group. However, your role is to observe the dynamics and see where a little change might help. For example, if you're a technical manager, you might see a team struggle to agree on a particular architecture or design. Your job isn't to decide *for* the team. Your job is to create an environment where the team can find a way to decide. I'll explain more about this in Managers Can Help Unstick Problem-Solving on page 31.

You might think your job is to manage everyone's work. That's not a manager's role. Managers create the environment in which the people they serve can succeed. Management is a specialization of leadership.

In most of my management jobs, I didn't have time to do any technical work. If I had tried to do that work, I would not have been a successful manager. I valued management enough that I learned how to delegate.

As a first-level manager, the more technical work I delegated, the more successful I became. I sometimes offered my coaching, when I still knew about the work. However, I often asked the person having trouble if they knew of someone who could coach them. They did. I facilitated the coaching experience. I didn't do the coaching when I was no longer sufficiently technical.

As a middle manager, the more I worked with the managers I served to solve problems, the more successful I became. I used the same coaching stance—I coached where I could and offered to help find someone where I could not.

And, as a senior manager, I made sure the managers I served understood the strategy, the purpose, and our constraints. That's how we succeeded. I often coached middle managers about how they could facilitate other teams and people to complete the work.

Managers often need to help themselves and others learn or explore other options. That's coaching. Once people see they have another option, they need time to experiment, so they can practice these new skills.

Every person needs to learn at their own pace. A coach might help the person see other options. And, implementing those options requires self-learning. People don't learn new skills in one day—every skill takes time and practice to master.

When you solve problems, the people you serve can see *your* solutions. They might not see your thinking, but they see solutions.

When you practice delegation, you might not be able to see how others think about the problems. They might solve problems differently—maybe even better than you did. If they do, rejoice in their success. Then, you can learn what they saw so you can incorporate that knowledge into your work. If you're worried about people doing it "wrong," consider instead ways to think about how to delegate and catch people doing the work right. (See Are You the One to Solve This

Problem? on page 27 and Does Your Team Need You So They Can Work? on page 35 for more details about coaching and delegation.)

Too many people think managers know it "all" or need to know it all. Nope. That's impossible.

Managers are human. Managers clarify the purpose or set the strategy or direction. Managers help teams and groups create the environment in which they can succeed. Managers see where people need to learn and enable that learning.

That means managers don't succeed by controlling other people's actions. Managers can only succeed if they see themselves and manage their actions and reactions.

1.6 Consider These Principles for Managing Yourself

When managers manage themselves first, they adapt the principles in these ways:

1. Clarify your purpose so you can serve others. As a manager, you provide value by creating an environment that makes it possible for people to do their best work.
2. Build empathy with the people who do the work. Learn what makes them tick and realize people live up or down to your expectations. You see how they can contribute to the whole and how they might grow to contribute more.
3. Build a safe environment. Psychological and physical safety matter. People can discuss and experiment in a safe environment. They tend to trust and respect each other more.
4. Seek outcomes and optimize for the overarching goal. When you delegate problems and outcomes, all for the purpose of the overarching goal, the team can decide how to engage in that challenging work.
5. Encourage experiments and learning. When you decriminalize mistakes, you can admit when you are wrong. That encourages

other people to admit when they are wrong—and to ask for help. That one admission can create a culture of experimentation and learning.

6. Catch people succeeding. When you admit you don't know and when you take time to think, you can see where people succeed—often, without you. People can build on their successes—and so can you.
7. Exercise your value-based integrity as a model for the people you lead and serve.

You'll notice I didn't include transparency or communication in these principles. That's because if you use all these principles, you will communicate effectively. You will be as transparent as you can be with the people you serve.

You create an environment where people can do their best work.

Given these principles, consider how you can build your management excellence.

1.7 Build Your Management Excellence

I've practiced some form of management for more than 35 years. I've managed inside organizations as an employee and as a contract manager. I've led volunteer organizations in a variety of leadership positions. I've managed myself as a consultant for the past 25 years.

I've coached managers, consulted to managers, and led leadership and management workshops.

I've worked with some super-smart people who did not realize that their management actions led to reactions exactly opposite of what they wanted. These people repeated the "typical" management practices they'd learned, or that HR requested, or that their own managers used on them.

These people wondered why they didn't get the results they wanted. You might be one of these people, too.

Management—especially congruent management—can create an environment in which everyone works to the best of their abilities.

Congruent managers balance the needs of everyone: yourself, the various others, and the context. That's management excellence.

Incongruent management often causes people to respond to incentives, fear, or some numeric target. People are smart. If you reward or create fear for a certain kind of action, people will act to achieve the reward or avoid the fear. These people won't necessarily want to work that way, or feel good about their work, but they will act in response to the rewards or fear.

When you manage yourself first, you can then ask people to be the best versions of themselves, all day, every day. You'll see what people are capable of—including yourself.

I've framed each of these chapters as questions for several reasons:

- I'm asking you to consider alternatives for your current behaviors. Questions help create divergent thinking, so we can consider alternatives. (For more information, see *A More Beautiful Question: The Power of Inquiry to Spark Breakthrough Ideas* [BER14].)
- My suggestions might not fit you or your context. How can you adapt my questions to your context?
- Questions might help you see different actions.

I'm not asking you to change your beliefs. Your beliefs arise from the results of your actions and interactions with others. If I can suggest an experiment for you—and you try it—you're more likely to subsequently change your belief.

Management excellence doesn't mean you need to be perfect. No one is perfect all the time. You can practice the management skills that lead to congruence and management excellence.

Become a modern manager and build ease in your management, starting with how you manage yourself.

CHAPTER 2

How Valuable Are Managers?

I used to joke that managers got paid the big bucks to make decisions. Back when I worked for a hardware-software company, one of the people I served asked me how much money I made. I was a little surprised and then answered him.

He was a senior architect and earned about 30% more than I did. Neither of us had bonuses. It was all straight pay.

He was quite surprised. “Why don’t you make more money if you’re more valuable than I am?”

I said, “We’re both valuable. You’re making design decisions that are quite costly to change and that will last a long time. The cost of change for your decisions is quite high.”

He nodded. “That’s true. My design decisions last many years,” he said.

I continued. “The decisions I make are much less costly to change. I can change my mind and not screw up the company’s future.”

He frowned. “But you hire people. If we hire a bad person, that screws everything up.”

“True,” I said. “And, I can assess their value as soon as they start. I can offer feedback. I can coach the people who work with a supposedly bad person to offer feedback. And I always have the option of firing that person. I’m not afraid of acting sooner rather than later to correct a difficult situation.”

He laughed. “Yup, you’re not afraid more than anyone I’ve met.” He paused. “That alone makes you more valuable than other managers.”

"Thanks," I said. "When I think about the value of a person, I think about the cost of their decisions and the cost of change. Sometimes, managers are more valuable. But not always."

I hope you think about the value of your work as you read the following myth.

2.1 Myth: I Am More Valuable than Other People

Belinda, the VP of Engineering, gathered her thoughts. *I am not looking forward to this conversation, but I need to have it. Again.*

Dan, the Director of Development, arrived on time for his one-on-one. "Hey, Belinda. Do you think we need all of our time? I have another meeting in ten minutes."

Belinda frowned. "I'm pretty sure we'll need all of our time. Do you want to tell anyone that you won't be there on time?"

Dan shrugged. "They'll wait for me."

"I hope not," Belinda said. "I have a number of things on my list." Belinda stood up and grabbed her notes and notebook. She walked over to her visitor's table and sat down with Dan. "What's been going on this week with you and your teams?"

They discussed the problems that Dan's teams had solved and what remained.

Dan then said, "I have to tell you, I'm really enjoying this new role."

"Oh? Tell me more."

"Well, I get to tell people what to do. I really get to boss people around."

"Do you find that effective?" Belinda asked. "Can you provide me with some examples of how that works for you?"

"Sure," Dan replied. "In the Alpha project, I told that team, you know, the one with Vijay, Susie, and those two other people whose names I can't remember? Well, I told them to get off their tushes and get down to business. We can't wait all day for them to 'spike' their work. We need results. And what did they do? They finished their work. I sure told them." Dan preened.

Belinda paused for a minute. "Dan, do you remember anything about developing software?"

"Sure, but my needs are so much more valuable now. You asked me for an estimate. I gave you an estimate, right?"

"Yes, but what you gave me was meaningless," Belinda said. "You intimidated the team. You threw your weight around and acted like a bully. You can't even remember the names of all the people who work for you."

Dan leaned back and crossed his arms. He arched one eyebrow.

"I don't want a single-point estimate," Belinda said. "That's not useful. I want something I can work with, but that's not the point here."

Dan arched the other eyebrow.

"When you disregard the fact that people work hard to provide you good data, you belittle their work," Belinda said. "You might not like the way these people work, but that's not up to you. They have chosen to work that way, and as long as they produce results, they can choose to work that way."

Dan opened his mouth as if to say something.

"I've got more," Belinda said. "When you don't know the names of the people you serve, you act as if you are more valuable than the people in your group. You're not acting as a servant leader, which is what I need from my managers. Great managers serve the people who work for them. Yes, they also serve their managers. Middle managers are stuck in the middle. I serve my managers, and I serve you, which is why I'm offering you this feedback."

Dan shook his head slowly. "I'm not so sure I know what you mean."

"Okay," Belinda said. "When you tell people to stop spiking, what do you think will happen?"

Dan's eyebrows came together. He frowned. "They'll just get on with the work, right?"

"Well, they might. If they do, they have no idea how long something will take. If you then ask for an estimate, it will serve you right if they answer 'Christmas' and don't tell you *which* Christmas. I bet these smart people will ignore you and continue doing whatever they were doing before. You will marginalize yourself."

"I'm doing that?"

"Yes. The problem is that managers are not *more* valuable than technical people. You can't believe your own press. Managers provide different value."

Dan started to shake his head. "What do you mean 'believe your own press'?"

"Look," Belinda said. "You can use that manager title to tell people what to do. You can tell them how big the estimate should be. You can tell them any number of things, and the telling might even work for a while. However, when you do that, you're telling people how to think. What do you think could happen?"

Dan tapped his fingers on the table. "Well, they might stop telling me what *they* think."

Belinda nodded. "Worse, they might stop thinking altogether and wait for you to decide about almost anything useful."

Dan sighed.

Belnda said, "Managers are valuable when they serve their teams. Managers are valuable when they create an environment in which people can solve problems. Managers are *not* valuable when they puff out their chests and say, 'Look at me, I'm the manager.' When you put your needs first, you are not helping anyone."

Dan sat there, stunned. "But you gave me all these responsibilities for projects. I have to deliver them."

"*You* don't deliver the projects. You facilitate the teams to deliver the projects. You have management responsibilities to create and refine the environment so people can do the work."

"I thought I had more responsibilities."

"You do. Management responsibilities differ from delivering the work," Belinda said. "Especially as a middle manager."

Dan nodded. "My work isn't the same as when I managed one team," he said.

"Middle managers 'deliver' when they work through their teams," Belinda said. "You don't do them yourself. That's why you have people who deliver the actual products and services, the work. You ask people how long the work might take, right? You decide on the project portfolio, along with the other directors and me, because we make decisions as a management team. You help your teams problem-solve. You provide meta-feedback and meta-coaching. If people ask you to remove management obstacles, you do so. That's how you can manage the fifty to sixty people you have in your group—through your managers. How else could you manage that many people?"

Dan crossed his arms again.

"Look, you serve the teams—the people. They don't serve you. Just because you have a title with 'director' in it does not make you 'more' than anyone else. Your title means your decisions are more strategic for the organization. Other people make strategic product decisions. You might help with those, too, but you are not more valuable than they are."

"Well, I never thought about management like that," Dan said.

Belinda smiled. "Would you like to talk some more about what management is?"

2.2 Middle Managers Have a Difficult Balancing Act

Many middle managers find themselves in tricky situations. They have a senior manager who says, "Gimme this project," or "Deliver that report," or "Do this with half the time/budget/people." That senior manager—and often the middle manager—is too far from the technical work to understand the details of it. They resort to mandates, demands, or blaming the project teams because they don't understand what it takes to deliver a product.

We have all seen the demands roll downhill and the environment that creates. It's not pretty. It's incongruent.

Any of those behaviors—mandates, demands, blaming—are all signs of incongruence. At the very least, managers who mandate, demand, or blame miss the other person in the interaction. Too often, they also miss the context. These managers only think of themselves and how things affect their own situation.

2.3 Great Management Is Servant Leadership

When managers think of themselves and not the other or the context, they are rarely proactive when it comes to great servant leadership. (See Managers Serve and Lead Others on page 9.)

When I acted as an order-taker from my managers, I could not retain my personal integrity. You might feel the same.

It's a lot more work, but when managers understand what *their* managers want (i.e., the problem) and then provide solutions, organizations run better. For example, you might need to first clarify the overarching purpose for this work. You might not be able to create perfection, but you can create a better environment for the people you lead and serve.

Managers can create an environment where the team can solve the problems. That's the role of the servant leader.

It's not about managers being more or less valuable than the rest of the team; all team members contribute in their own way. What is important is *how* managers contribute. If managers don't provide servant leadership, they don't provide the leverage for everyone else. They are not creating an environment in which people can do their best work.

Bossing people around doesn't sound like valuable management to me. Does it sound that way to you?

Here's how I often think about valuable management: reducing the cost of a decision or the cost of change from those decisions.

2.4 Assess the Cost of Your Decisions or the Cost of Change

Your organization may well expect you to boss other people around. When you tell other people what to do, you make decisions *for* them. See more at Identify Your Delegation Boundaries on page 44.

What if your organization wants you to boss other people around? First, decide if that fits your ideas about management. You might want to review Managers Serve and Lead Others on page 9.

How much experience do the people you serve have with making decisions? Many organizations have a culture of bossing people around. You might have to support your team or group with facilitation coaching so they learn how to decide together.

Now that you've thought about yourself and the other, think of the context.

Consider these measures: what did it cost in time for *you* to make a decision? How long did it take for you to recognize you needed to change the decision? If that decision was ill-advised, what did it cost you to change that decision?

Think back to your last couple of weeks of work. Make a list of your answers to these questions:

- How often did you arrive late to a meeting? How long did the other people have to wait? This is the meeting wait time cost.
- How many times did you override a decision a person or a team made because you were the manager? This is a cost of insufficient trust.
- How long did people have to wait for your decision for a specific problem? This is a real Cost of Delay, due to the problem of Indispensable Employees Create Bottlenecks on page 126.

You might see other examples of delay-based costs.

Maybe you couldn't help being late to all those meetings. Maybe you had to override the original decisions. Maybe you needed more data to make a decision for that particular problem.

I'm not suggesting your actions or decisions were wrong. Your actions and decisions might have been exactly right. I am suggesting you're increasing the cost of your decisions with those delays. Each delay increases the risks in your system of work.

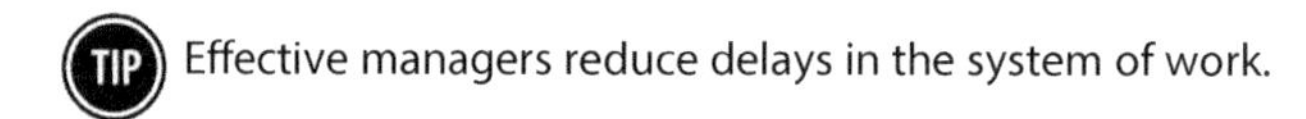

My question is this: Is there a way you can reduce the cost of your decisions? Try to imagine ways to:

- Delegate more decisions so you don't have to participate in as many meetings? See Does Your Team Need You So They Can Work? on page 35.
- Extend more trust. See How Much Do You Trust the People You Serve? on page 115.
- Be less indispensable as a problem solver. See Are You the One to Solve This Problem? on page 27.

The longer it takes to make a decision, the less likely we are to reassess that decision. That's the Sunk Cost Fallacy—we spend so much time and invest so much emotionally in a decision that we don't want to change our minds.

The more decisions we are reluctant to change, the more fragile the system of work becomes. (See *Antifragile: Things That Gain from Disorder* [TAL12] for more details.) The more decisions you make, the fewer chances other people have to make decisions. With those fewer chances, people learn less from their decisions. Although you might appear more valuable in the short term, your ability to work through other people diminishes over time.

You may have experienced these consequences of appearing to be more valuable:

- At some point, what you know will no longer be useful. Your knowledge has a shelf life.
- You will have a difficult time creating a succession plan if you want to move around in the organization.
- The people you serve will not have the capability of managing their own work if you solve problems for them.

Refer back to your list of the times people waited for your decisions. Then ask yourself:

- Am I the only one who can make these decisions? If so, do you have options to help other people learn to make these decisions?
- Are these decisions relatively easy to change as we learn more? If they are, maybe do nothing until you know more.
- Have I waited too long to make decisions? If so, what would you need to do to make a decision closer to the time everyone needs the decision?

When is the last responsible and *reasonable* time you and everyone else can make a decision?

2.5 Consider the Value You Offer

Where do you offer value? Do you coach team members or teams? Do you clear organizational problems and impediments so the teams and team members can do their work? Do you see the various needs for education or training and then arrange that training?

Here are some ideas for thinking about the value you offer to the organization:

1. How many people have you unwedged or unblocked this week? Sometimes team members may not realize they are stuck trying to solve problems. If you are able to recognize that someone is stuck and point them in a more useful direction, then you've accomplished valuable work.

2. How many of the people you serve were able to accomplish more based on decisions you made or impediments you cleared? When you do that, you offer leverage to others.
3. How much strategic work did you do this week? Managers set the strategy for their teams and groups. Then they put the tactics in place to make the work happen. Strategic goals are long-term goals, so you'd expect to make only a little progress on strategic work each week. But the effort you invest and the progress you make certainly count.
4. How many crises did you prevent? Every time you solve a problem and prevent a disaster or crisis, you've given the people you serve ways to progress.
5. How many meetings were you able to cancel? Unfortunately, too many of us work in meeting-happy organizations. If you are able to cancel meetings that don't actually help move a project forward, then you've done wonderful management work.

You might offer value in other ways. As you read through this book—and with any luck, the other two books—you might see ways to offer more value to the people, the customers, and the organization.

Valuable managers balance the time they spend in the work with the time they spend creating the environment for other people to do great work.

Consider how much time you spend *in* the work rather than on the system of work.

CHAPTER 3

Are You the One to Solve This Problem?

Many managers got promoted because they excelled at their jobs. They might have excelled as a team member. Or, they might have managed one team and now manage managers.

Their promotions mean their management roles offer more value to the organization—and require more responsibility.

However, managers who continue to solve problems at their previous level create problems for those who now have that responsibility. Those problems are now other people's problems.

Great managers don't solve other people's problems for them. Great managers resist the temptation to jump in and inflict help. Too many managers inflict help because the manager needs the ego boost. "I need to know I did *something* today."

Managers create an environment in which everyone can succeed. That is the manager's job. Sometimes, it doesn't feel like that's "real" work. But it is.

When managers see problems and jump to conclusions, they prevent the people or the team from solving the problems on their own. This is a form of micromanagement: unhealthy and incongruent management.

3.1 Myth: I Must Solve the Team's Problem for Them

Josiah, the new VP of engineering, called his directors' meeting to order. "First on our agenda is my plan for the reorganization of our department," he said.

The directors looked at each other, puzzled.

"I've noticed that several of the project teams are having trouble working together, so I've decided that we need a reorganization back to functional teams."

After a couple of seconds of shocked silence, Dave, the QA Director said, "Oh, no, don't even think about going there. Don't take a step backward like that. If you do, I don't know what we will do with our test and measurement effort."

Cheryl, the Development Director, said, "Right, our development is finally making forward progress with test-driven development (TDD) and with continuous integration. Don't even think about making siloed teams. The teams have conflict. They are working it out. Leave them alone. What problems are you trying to solve? Why are you thinking about doing this?"

Josiah replied, "Wait a minute. I saw some significant discussions last week. I thought those discussions looked a lot like arguments. I thought Charlie and Sharon were going to actually fight it out. And I thought Tranh and Dan were going to beat each other up in the parking lot when I saw them discussing the design of that feature earlier this week. If we break up the developers and testers into functional groups, they won't fight as often, right?

Cheryl looked at Dave. "You want to take this?"

"Yes, thank you," Dave said. "Josiah, the testers and developers are finally learning how to work together. And now that the business analysts are on the teams, too, and the teams have acceptance criteria for the stories, everyone is involved from the beginning. This is new for the teams. They have never worked this way before. You need to expect growing pains. People are frustrated. That's fine."

Josiah stood up and leaned over, his hands on the table. "How is their frustration *fine*?" His voice increased in volume with every word.

Cheryl said, "Let them work it out. We, the managers, are working with the teams, coaching people individually, providing feedback, helping them create a safe environment in which to work. If you come in and mess with the system, we will have to start all over again."

Josiah cocked his head and sat down.

Cheryl said, "Oh, you didn't realize we created psychological safety in the teams, and between us as managers?"

Josiah said, "No."

Dave said, "Oh, nuts. We worked really hard with the teams and with us as a team. You meshed really well with us this past month. We didn't even think about creating a team with *you.*"

Josiah said, "I should have thought of that. No wonder I didn't understand what I was seeing."

Cheryl hit her forehead with her palm. "Sorry about that. Until you said 'reorganize,' I thought we had integrated you into our thinking. Let's talk more about why we don't want to reorganize."

Dave continued. "We'll still have the same *project* teams. But with functional teams, people will have to run around to find each other. That will make their lives much more difficult."

Cheryl took over. "These people are adults. All of us in this room have made ourselves available to our people. We all have one-on-ones. We have facilitated communities of practice. We have been helping people with their feedback skills and their coaching skills. We are not solving their problems *for* them. We are monitoring their issues, and if we need to, we will step in. Make sense?"

Josiah rocked a little in his chair. "Oh boy. I'm going to trust you, but we need more transparency so I understand how things are working."

Cheryl nodded. "We can do that. We'll show you our quantitative and qualitative metrics. You can see how we're doing and we'll keep earning your trust."

Dave said, "Okay, we've taken care of that item. Now, what's next on your list?"

3.2 Managers Want to Be Helpful

Everyone wants to be helpful. That includes managers, middle managers, and senior managers. But the more managers interfere with a team's growth, the less a team learns how to perform.

When a team learns how to perform differently—in this case, transitioning to an agile approach—managers need to expect a transition time where people experience a variety of changes in their performance and their emotions. This is okay. Managers need to support the change rather than changing things again.

Solving problems for the team does not help. Based on what the directors said, they focused on creating a supportive environment for the teams. They created a safe atmosphere in which the teams could work. The fact that Josiah even saw disagreements tells me that they succeeded.

Management help is often indirect. Instead of solving problems for people, managers help people learn how to solve the problems themselves.

The directors conducted one-on-ones and provided feedback and coaching so that people didn't work open-loop with no feedback. People knew where they stood with each other and with the team. The teams created psychological safety as teams. That is management help.

When managers persist in solving a team's problem for them, the managers infantilize the team and the team members. In addition, the managers ignore other people and the context. These managers only think of themselves and either their perceived problem-solving speed or the ego boost the solution will give the manager.

3.3 Encourage the People Who See the Problems to Solve Them

If you want to empower people or teams, make sure that the people with the problem solve the problem for themselves. If those people struggle with a problem for too long, then you might want to ask if they need help.

However, one of the ways managers can help is with problem-solving skills. Sometimes, teams or the people with the problem are so immersed in the problem that they have trouble seeing solutions.

3.4 Managers Can Help Unstick Problem-Solving

There's a quote attributed to Albert Einstein: "Problems cannot be solved by the same level of thinking that created them."

Managers can help when people are stuck in their same thinking. Managers can help because they can "go meta" and see the situation from the outside. Managers are not the only people who can do this, but sometimes managers are ideally placed to see the problems.

Going "meta" means thinking about the system that caused the problem rather than about the problem itself. When managers consider the system that caused the problem, the managers can coach the people or the team.

For me, coaching is about offering options with support. I don't start by telling people my opinions or the options *I* see. I explain the problem I see and make sure the person or the team sees the same problem. Once we agree on the situation and the data, I can help people get unstuck in how they approach solving the problem.

People often get stuck because they don't see useful options. One of the ways I like to help people or teams get unstuck is to generate options using the Rule of Three (from *Behind Closed Doors: Secrets of Great Management* [BCD05]):

What are three potential reasonable options to solve this problem?

One solution is a trap. Two solutions are a dilemma. Three alternatives help us see possibilities. In addition, the three alternatives might help people generate even more possibilities. We now have choices.

You can help people generate three reasonable options for a problem, especially if they are stuck on one option.

Aside from using the Rule of Three to generate options, managers can ask, "What would it look like if you did know how to solve this problem?" Yes, that's a funny question, but it sometimes works.

As a third option, ask, "What kind of help do you need from me?" It could be that the team has not thought of you as a resource for help. The team might need a facilitator. Or a whiteboard. Or a person to bounce ideas off of. Or something else. You, the manager, might be just what the team needs.

When managers coach instead of solve problems, the teams' capabilities increase. With increased capabilities and knowledge, the manager can catch people or teams doing the work right.

3.5 Let the Team Solve Its Own Problems

It's so tempting to get in the middle and inflict help on a team. After all, the manager has the organizational power to do so. But that doesn't make it right.

Facilitate the team's problem-solving. Provide the team with what it needs. And then stay out of the team's way. Every time I have done this, the team has developed a much better solution than anything I had considered—every single time.

Managers do not have to solve a team's problems. They can provide feedback, coaching, a meta-perspective, facilitation, or a problem-solving environment. But they rarely need to directly solve a problem *for* the team. Before you solve a problem for a team, ask yourself, "Am I doing this for me or for the team?"

3.6 Options to Avoid Inflicting Help

If you regularly interfere as soon as you see a problem, you might worry about how the team will solve its own problems. You might worry that the team needs your help.

Consider these options to recognize and avoid inflicting help:

- Explain, "I see this problem. Do you also see it?" If the person or team agrees that they also see the problem, you can then ask, "Do you understand the problem?" You might need to frame the problem or share risks the team hasn't yet considered.
- Ask, "Do you need any more information from me?"
- Use curiosity. "I wonder if you realize . . ." and explain your concern.
- Ask, "Do you need my help to solve this problem?"

Listen to the answers. The people you serve may be on the right track. Extend trust. If necessary, ask when they will explain their progress to you.

Make sure you're not solving the problem so you can feel good about your abilities. Great managers facilitate other people doing the work. I'll discuss psychological safety more in Book 2.

CHAPTER 4

Does Your Team Need You So They Can Work?

I meet many leaders who are afraid to take vacations or to totally break from the office when they do. These are the same people who take calls and other interrupts when they go to conferences or participate in workshops.

These managers allow the organization to interrupt them when they need to take a break, for vacation, learning, or even for a customer visit.

It doesn't matter where you are in the organization, you need to take a vacation. And you need to totally remove yourself from the day-to-day grind when you do.

No one is too valuable to take a vacation. Everyone needs time off to recharge and gain a new perspective. Don't think you are sacrificing yourself for the good of your team.

Taking a vacation will also help your team. It will help your team practice with various responsibilities—not forever, but at least for now.

Taking breaks from the office allows you to:

- Learn with other people at workshops;
- Learn from and with other people at conferences;
- Expand your network so you can hire people more easily; and
- Gain perspective, especially if you take a vacation. We often see a situation differently when we're not in the middle of it.

While other breaks are a great idea, everyone needs a vacation. Here's what happens if you think you are too valuable to take a vacation.

4.1 Myth: I Am Too Valuable to Take a Vacation

I caught up with Fred, a longtime friend, just before what I thought would be his normal two- to three-week vacation in August. "Where are you going this year, Fred? Are you bicycling or white water rafting? Or something else exciting? I can't wait to live vicariously through you again!"

"I'm not going anywhere this year, JR," Fred said and frowned. "My team depends on me too much. I can't afford to take a vacation."

"Who said that?" I stood there with my mouth open in astonishment. "You need your vacations. They energize you. And people like me actually *want* to see your vacation pictures!"

"Nope. I've decided. I'm a manager now. If I take a vacation, who will make all the decisions? How will my team know what to do? I'll just stay here and make the sacrifice. No more vacations for me."

I still couldn't believe it. "Fred, are you sick? Did you lose all your money in the stock market? Did Jeannie leave you and take the children? Is there something seriously wrong?"

"No," he said in his best Eeyore[1] voice. "My team members depend on me. I can't let them down. I must support them. I must. I must." As Fred ambled down the hall, I stood there dumbfounded.

Fred is laboring under an all-too-common manager's myth—that they are the only drivers and decision makers for their teams. That's a dangerous belief.

First, it means that you can never delegate work to the team and be confident the team can complete the work. Second, it means you can never work yourself out of *this* job and into another one. Third, it's not true, regardless of the team or workgroup you manage, agile or not. Your team makes decisions without you all the time.

So, how did things get this way?

---

[1] Eeyore is a donkey in the *Winnie the Pooh* books. He expects things to go badly. He tends to be a martyr.

4.2 "Please Stay in Touch While You Are Gone"

When I first started to work, we didn't have cell phones or pagers. Long-distance calls were expensive. When we took vacations, we were gone, totally out of touch. That meant that regardless of our position in the organization, we had to explain to someone else the state of our work. It didn't matter whether I was a manager or not—-and for my first few vacations I most certainly was not—I had to explain to someone what I was working on and where my colleagues could find the necessary details.

In the same way, when my managers went on vacation, they delegated their management responsibilities to other people. Sometimes they chose an acting manager. Sometimes they spread their responsibilities around.

One year, my manager took a two-week vacation. I was the acting software support manager. Another fellow was the acting software development manager. A third colleague was the acting project manager. We didn't realize it, but it was a two-week long test to see if we could organize ourselves and get along with each other while our boss was on vacation. I'm delighted to say we passed!

These days, we have easy and inexpensive electronic access to each other. Most of the time, this is great. "Please stay in touch while you are gone," sounds like a harmless request, doesn't it? But it creates an environment for bad management because it allows us to be lazy about creating and maintaining our line between work and vacation.

When you stay in touch on your vacation, several problems occur:

1. You are not taking a real vacation to decompress and let yourself relax. A vacation is a chance to get away from all physical *and* electronic tethers to the office. If you're still tethered, you don't make the time to explain the state of all your work. Then you don't really decompress on vacation because at least a little part of your brain is still worrying about work.
2. You are not building a succession plan because you have not fully delegated specific work to your team members or your

boss. Vacations are a safe way to experiment with delegating some work. Without a succession plan, you can never move from this role to another in the organization. You are stuck.

3. Your team might think you don't trust them when you do not take the time to delegate specific work to your team members. Especially as team members grow, they expect to take on greater responsibilities. They expect you to delegate some of your work. You may not mean to imply that you don't trust them, but your actions say that you don't.
4. Your team or boss will appreciate your specific management problems. When you delegate your issues to team members, they have more empathy for your management problems. You may not be able to delegate all the issues to your team if the problem is sensitive in some way. You may have to delegate some of the issues to your boss, who might be surprised by some of your problems, too.
5. You lose the potential perspective you might gain from noodling your problems while you are not under a deadline. I find that when I put problems aside for a while and don't actively work on them, I return refreshed, with a new outlook. After a vacation, you might discover the same thing.
6. You lose the perspective that another person might provide on the problems you currently manage. Aside from gaining perspective on your problems while on vacation, other people see your problems differently. When you don't share your problems, you lose the opportunity to see how other people perceive them.

I've seen at least these problems. You might see more problems.

4.3 Do You Feel Indispensable?

When you believe you are indispensable, you act that way, which is never good for a manager. "Indispensable" managers insert themselves into situations and create messes.

I once worked as a project manager on a difficult machine vision project. There were three of us: Bruce (the other software person), and Charles, the mechanical engineer. We were pushing the state of the current technology to solve the problem.

The client was in another state. But we showed the client several interim deliverables, and the client was happy. I went on vacation—my honeymoon—and delegated my work to Bruce.

I was only absent from work for eight days, but the time off gave me the chance to think about the technical challenge from a fresh perspective. I was looking forward to discussing a possible new algorithm with Bruce when I returned.

When I returned, the technical problems were the least of my concerns.

While I was gone, a senior manager, Al, decided he was indispensable to the project. He assumed Bruce and Charles needed direct supervision. He decided the client needed daily updates. Al was wrong on all counts.

With his interference, Al destroyed the client relationship. He angered Charles to the point that Charles threatened to quit the day I returned.

Al assumed he was indispensable. I was unable to fire Al, but I did explain to him that I needed Charles to complete the project.

"Indispensable" managers remove their team's independence and insert themselves into situations they have no business being in. You might see development managers writing code or test managers testing. In my case, the senior manager attempted to act as a project manager and account manager.

When managers insert themselves into the work, they micromanage other people. Too often, they don't encourage alternative perspectives.

But managers are not paid to control the work or micromanage. Managers create leverage for the people doing the work, often by removing organizational problems. When Managers Manage the System on page 10, the teams or groups can do the technical work.

4.4 Prepare to Delegate

Before you take a vacation, ask yourself these questions:

1. Have I clarified the work I have delegated and to whom?
2. Does everyone know who has what responsibility?
3. Is the responsibility list posted somewhere, physically and electronically?

If you have explained who has all the various responsibilities, why would anyone need to know how to stay in touch with you? They don't. Unless you have not delegated all the work or if you have not clarified who has which roles and responsibilities.

4.5 Consider What You Can Delegate

If you're accustomed to leading the problem-solving and implementation of solutions for your team, consider all your management decision areas. Consider delegating all of these decisions to the people doing the work:

- Project practices, such as how to organize the project (for example, a serial, iterative, incremental, or agile approach), or how to rank the work. Encourage the team as a whole to manage its own work.
- Work practices, such as which tools to use in which circumstances. Encourage the team to experiment with their work practices.
- Technical practices, such as coding guidelines, coding, or test practices. Encourage the team to assess the various risks so they can create and use their own technical practices.

Explain the results you want, and let the people decide for themselves how to achieve those results. Teams can select the most reasonable practices when managers explain the desired results.

Most managers cannot delegate these decisions:

- People issues, such as hiring and firing. HR might need to be involved.
- Money issues: does anyone other than you have or need signature authority for any reason while you are gone?

In my experience, teams don't know how to hire, fire, or integrate new people. As a manager, you might *lead* the hiring and help people learn how to hire effectively. (See *Hiring Geeks That Fit* [ROT12].)

In addition, I meet too few teams that know how to offer feedback and coaching to each other. You might have to help people learn how. (See *Create Your Successful Agile Project: Collaborate, Measure, Estimate, Deliver* [ROT17] for specifics.)

The more the team or group can self-manage, the fewer of these areas need your oversight or control. For example, I don't see why managers would want to be involved in the technical practice decisions or many of the work practice decisions. Explain the results you want, and let the people decide for themselves.

If you want people to change how they work on projects, you might need to lead that change by asking for different deliverables. For example, if you want people to use an agile approach, you might have to ask them to manage their WIP (Work in Progress), or show you demos on a regular basis.

The people you serve might need *guidance*, especially if they want to spend money.

4.6 Support Your Team's Decisions

Let's assume you go on vacation. While you're gone, your team makes decisions that you don't agree with. What do you do then?

Support your team. Let the decision stand until the team wants to change the decision.

Let's imagine the team made what you think is a bad decision in areas the team controls, as in Consider What You Can Delegate on page 40: project practices, work practices, or technical practices. What's the worst thing that could happen? They might take longer to finish work. They might have more quality problems.

Instead of changing any of those decisions, consider asking them to measure their work.

If you're worried about the project practices in terms of bottlenecks or the time the team takes to finish the work, explain what you're worried about. Ask the team to measure their cycle time. You would do that even if you hadn't gone on vacation. Why? Because it's your job to help the team see the system. Maybe the team has an alternative you didn't consider.

Maybe the team changed their work practices and are now using a different tool. If the tool meets your organization's security needs and the tool meets their needs, why do you care? I understand each organization has to be careful with the security of all their digital bits. But, if the tool meets the security needs and meets the team's needs, let the decision stand.

Maybe your team changed their technical practices while you were gone. One infamous team decided to stop code reviews. They started to mob. That meant they no longer needed standups or code reviews.

The manager had never been part of a mob and worried they were not going to be able to maintain their high level of code and test quality. He was also worried they would not be as productive as they had been before. He was quite surprised when the product became more reliable and easier to change. He was also quite surprised that the team's throughput increased.

As a manager, why would you change any of those decisions? You might be wrong when it comes to how the team works. That's okay. Even if you cannot imagine a better way, your team can. And when you provide autonomy to the team, everyone can succeed.

Always support your team's decisions.

Support your team in their decisions. Even if you didn't take a vacation. You only have to reverse a team's decision once. And they will never again make a decision when you're gone.

Sometimes you have done everything right. But your managers are not accustomed to managers who have delegated well, and they question your decisions and your team's decisions.

4.7 Avoid Anyone Second Guessing Your Team's Decisions

If you suspect that other people will question your team's decisions and will want to contact you, you may have to prepare an email or memo in advance, not just a list of who is responsible for what.

That email might look something like this:

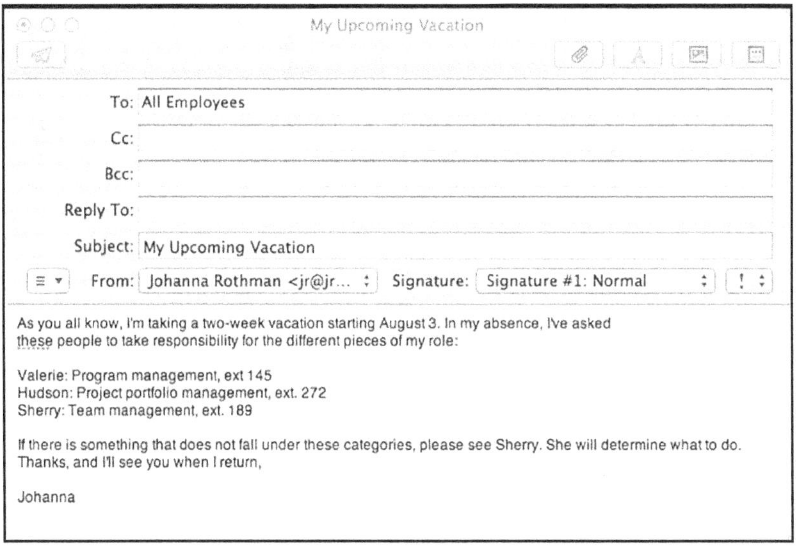

My Upcoming Vacation

To: All Employees
Cc:
Bcc:
Reply To:
Subject: My Upcoming Vacation
From: Johanna Rothman <jr@jr... Signature: Signature #1: Normal

As you all know, I'm taking a two-week vacation starting August 3. In my absence, I've asked these people to take responsibility for the different pieces of my role:

Valerie: Program management, ext 145
Hudson: Project portfolio management, ext. 272
Sherry: Team management, ext. 189

If there is something that does not fall under these categories, please see Sherry. She will determine what to do.
Thanks, and I'll see you when I return,

Johanna

Figure 4.1: Vacation email

If you have more responsibilities, your email will be longer. Maybe you don't need to send your email to everyone; maybe you only need to send it to a few people. Use your judgment, but make sure that you send the email to everyone who might question your team's decisions.

Just as you will support your team's decisions, your peers or managers need to support their decisions, too.

When you learn to delegate and delegate successfully, you exhibit congruent management. You're taking each person, you, and the context into account.

4.8 Identify Your Delegation Boundaries

You can't delegate everything to the team. You will need to set boundaries about what to delegate and how. I already discussed some of the "what" in Consider What You Can Delegate on page 40.

Then there's the "how" to delegate. Decisions have several parts.

- Who decides when it's time to address an issue or solve a problem? Does the team decide when? Do you decide when?
- Who sets the boundaries around the issue or solution? Are there guidelines or rules you need to clarify, such as timeliness, cost, or a specific outcome?
- Who identifies the possible options? Do you need to generate the options, or can the team?
- Who evaluates the options?
- Who selects from the options? Are there criteria you need to use?
- Who implements the decision?
- If you need an evaluation step after implementation, who evaluates the work? You might think of this as a kaizen or retrospective.

There are at least two possible answers to each question: the manager or the team. The more often your answer is "the manager," the less self-managing your team can be. The more often your answer is "the team," the more self-managing your team is.

Sometimes, you need the team to identify options and prepare their evaluation. Then you, as the manager, will select an option. The team might implement the decision, and all of you will evaluate it.

Clarify how much of the decision making is theirs and how much is yours. I like thinking about a continuum of delegation options, especially if you and the team don't have a lot of practice with delegating decisions.

On the far left of the continuum in Figure 4.2, you *tell* people what your decision is. You might have a responsibility for money that you cannot delegate at all.

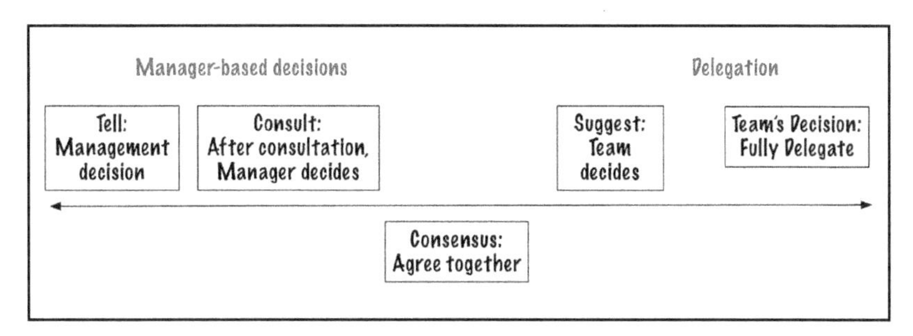

Figure 4.2: Decision Autonomy Continuum

To the right of that is where you consult with the team. You will make the final decision, but you ask for the team's opinion.

Consensus, in the middle, is where you and the team decide together. I use limited consensus for hiring decisions. I *want* full consensus for a hiring decision. But, sometimes, the team can't agree. If no one is opposed to the candidate, I'll extend an offer to the candidate. That's an example of limited consensus.

To the right of consensus, you suggest. If you ever offer a strawman option and leave the decision to the team, then you have suggested.

Full delegation is all the way on the right. Refer back to Consider What You Can Delegate on page 40 for ideas. Consider the decision-making speed your team needs. The faster they need to decide, the more they need you to delegate as many decisions as possible.

Ask yourself this question: How self-managing can your team be?

If your team typically evaluates options, selects one, and implements it, what would it be like to ask the team to start earlier? End later? What risks would you have to manage to make it safe for the team to experiment and for you to be comfortable?

Clarify how much of the decision-making is theirs and how much is yours. The less practice you have with delegation and the less practice the team has with taking decisions, the more practice you all need. Start with something small to manage the risks.

For a given decision, explain where you are in your thinking. Then stick to that, or explain why you were wrong.

Don't yank decisions back if you don't like the decision the team made, especially if you're not doing the work.

Congruent managers find a balance between insufficient delegation and not managing. If you don't delegate enough, you might placate other people. "I couldn't possibly ask them to do more work." If you don't support your team when they make a decision you disagree with, you blame them for doing something wrong.

It's true, delegation might be tricky to start. Maybe start with the following experiments and options.

4.9 Options to Start Delegation

If you're totally integrated into your team's work, you might feel uneasy about taking a vacation next week or next month, before you've practiced delegation.

Consider these options as practice for a vacation:

- Visit a customer for a day and delegate the various work you would normally be responsible for. Prepare the people you want to delegate the work to. Create working agreements about when they should contact you and when they shouldn't.
- Go to a two- or three-day workshop or conference. Again, prepare the delegation work.
- Consider an off-site with your entire team to work on the who-does-what issues and what people need to learn. I recommend you take an entire day for this, but maybe you can start with a half-day in a conference room. When you "delegate" the entire team's work, you might learn more about who expects what from the entire team.

Once you start to delegate, consider these reflection questions. Ask the team:

1. What decisions did you make that I normally make?
2. What decisions could you *not* make because I was not here?

The first question might show you where you prevent the team from doing their work. The second question helps you see where you have taken too much work from the team. You can practice delegating that work so it's easier for the team the next time.

As you start to delegate more work and decisions, try to catch people doing the work right.

Whatever you do, take your vacations. You will gain perspective, and your team members will gain practice and stretch their current capabilities. You all win.

4.10 Take a Vacation

You don't need to fear a vacation.

Want to really treat your team members well? Discuss how you make decisions now. See what you and they are willing to manage. Experiment and delegate more. You might discover that your team is much more self-managing than you had imagined.

And, all because you had the guts to take a vacation. Imagine that!

CHAPTER 5

Can You Be Effective as a Player-Coach?

Many senior managers believe a first-level manager can work as a player-coach. Too many first-level managers and senior technical people believe that, too.

If we continue the sports metaphor, how many coaches do you see who play as well as the people on the team? While many coaches are physically fit, they're not as fit as their players.

The "players"—here, the knowledge workers—excel at the tactical decisions. The developers in the code excel at design and architecture decisions, both small and large. The testers excel at seeing risks and providing information about the system under test.

The coaches—the managers—can excel at seeing the big picture, the system. The managers see the flow of information and where the bottlenecks are in the team or the project. The managers see the feedback loops and delays. The managers might even see the product strategy in ways the team members don't.

In the software industry, we've been burned by managers who didn't understand how to see the flow of information at all levels: in the team, between teams, between the parts of the organization. They especially didn't understand the relationship between the customers and the organization.

When managers don't understand the flow of information and the various relationships between the people involved, the managers cannot create a strategy for anything. Not for this team, project, program, or product. Certainly not for the organization itself.

Too many organizations have people who think, "A professional manager can manage anything." Nope. Not at all true. The domain matters. Managers who don't understand the domain can't see the system of work and the various risks.

While I am terrific at software and other technology management, I would need help to manage construction. I am a technical person, and I don't understand enough about the domain of construction to be an effective manager.

Effective managers understand the system of what they manage. They don't have to be super technical, but they do have to understand the system.

When we misunderstand the role of management, we believe the manager can be a player-coach and still do significant technical work. That's wishful thinking.

This myth is related to the various other delegation problems: not taking a vacation, feeling indispensable, and this problem of being a player-coach.

Here is a tip for managers:

Once you delegate something, do not take it back.

When we, as managers, see a technical problem, it's tempting to want to wade in and help—either by fixing the problem ourselves or by telling people how to fix it. But that destroys the trust we have built with our teams. Once we delegate the problems to the team, we need to leave the problem delegated.

If you're worried about being a hands-off manager, think about the times you've asked the team to deliver outcomes. I'll talk more about this in Book 2.

If you try to take technical problems back, you are not doing your team any favors. They will eventually stop trying to solve problems, anticipating your lack of delegation. Why should they solve problems if they know you are going to grab the problems back once things get sticky?

5.1 Myth: I Can Still Do Significant Technical Work

"You know, if you want something done, you just have to do it yourself," Clive muttered as he strode down to his office.

Susan looked up from her desk and sighed. She stood, followed Clive down the hall, and knocked on his office door.

"What? I'm a little busy right now!" he replied and turned back to his computer. Then, he turned to Susan and said, "Explain this part of the framework to me."

"No."

He looked at her, raised what Susan thought of as his "Spock" eyebrow. "No?" he asked. "You know I'm your boss."

Susan grinned. "You're right," she said. "You're the manager, but you're not asking me as my manager. You're asking me as someone who's going to go in and do some damage, as opposed to helping. How long have we known each other?" Clive sighed. "Ten years? Maybe more?"

"Yup," Susan said. "I had my ten-year anniversary last month. Remember when you said I was the calming influence on you?"

"Yes."

"Here's why," she said. "I'm the technical lead. If you have a problem with what's going on technically, you're supposed to talk to me. You're supposed to talk to the team. Why are you not talking to me? Why are you not talking to the team? Why are you messing with the code?"

Clive snorted. "Did you see what Todd did?"

"Yes."

"You can stand there calmly and say yes? You're not freaking out?" he asked.

"No, I'm not freaking out, because the team and I solved this problem this morning, which is more than you have done. Whose problem is this to solve?"

Clive took his fingers off the keyboard. "Uh, yours and the team's."

"Thank you. And did you ask me or the team how we were solving the problem?"

"Uh, no."

"So, you missed that Todd and Cindy are pairing on the fix for this problem, that we already have a patch on the production server, and that Dick and Samara are pairing on performance test development so we can catch this in the future. You missed all of that, right? Oh, and that we will be reviewing the code and the tests, right? You missed that?"

"Uh, yes."

"You were going to put on your Superman coder cape, and do it all yourself?"

"Uh, yes."

Susan sighed. Then she grinned. "Look, Clive, you were the Superman developer back in the day, but your day was more than five years ago. Even if it had been a year ago, you wouldn't know what we've done with the code. You cannot possibly be current with what we are doing. Back when you were active in the code, you were part of one five-person team, right?"

Clive nodded. "Yup, just five of us."

Susan nodded. "That's what I thought. We now have five teams of six people each. And, we've changed all the automated tests. And, we use different frameworks than you had access to all those years ago. You don't know what we're doing and what we're not doing any longer. You cannot do significant technical work anymore without doing real damage. Stop thinking you can."

Clive sighed. "But, what can I do to help when I see a problem?" he asked.

"Ask me what we need. Ask the team what we need. Make sure we are fed and watered," Susan said and grinned again. "Mostly, just ask. We'll tell you. Give us moral support, but don't mess with the code."

Clive started to nod, slowly.

Susan stood up to leave and said, "Oh, I've revoked your check-in privileges. You can read anything you want. You can't check anything in. And, I've changed the root password. You can't mess with anything technical. You're a manager. Be one."

Clive nodded again. "Probably about time," he said. "Susan, I'm going to want details until this is really all fixed."

"No problem, boss!" she said.

5.2 Do You Still Understand the Details?

Now, be honest with yourself. Do you still understand all the details of your team's technical work?

As soon as we become managers, our *technical* problem-solving skills start to erode. At least they *should* if we work on our management skills. Why? Because managers spend more time with people on the team and with other managers and less time with the code, the tests, the requirements, or whatever functional part of the organization you came from.

That doesn't mean we shouldn't know whom to ask about a problem, but we shouldn't know about all the technical details.

Once, when I was a Director of Development, a developer rushed into my office with a highly technical problem that he thought I could solve. I listened to make sure I understood his concerns. I knew I couldn't pinpoint where the problems were in the code.

However, the performance team had changed several aspects of performance the previous week. I could steer him to the correct people because I remained current with discussions. But I couldn't solve the problem.

If you don't understand the details anymore, is it your job to wade into the details? No, it's not. You can facilitate problem-solving. Do not solve the problems yourself.

5.3 Know What You Can Do

The best thing we can do as managers is to create an environment in which people can do their best work. Sometimes that means facilitating a problem-solving meeting. Sometimes it means making sure they have enough servers or debuggers or whiteboards. Sometimes it means keeping other people such as *your* manager out of the way.

Congruent managers will consider the needs of everyone—not just themselves—when they think about their role in the products and services your team provides.

5.4 Consider the Role of a Technical Manager

To paraphrase Peter Drucker, managers exist to organize with purpose. They organize people or help people organize themselves into project teams or workgroups. They organize problem-solving or project-solving teams. They organize ideas. Sometimes, they organize coffee, bagels, or pizza.

Managers see the flow of information, the work, and the people. When managers have perspective on the situation, they can help everyone solve problems.

5.5 Create an Environment Where People Can Solve Problems

Managers rarely solve the team's problems for them. Managers create an environment where people can solve their problems. As a manager, consider these options:

- Create a community of practice so people can learn together informally. That might mean finding funds for a book club. It might mean arranging space for "Lunch-and-Learn" meetings. It might mean asking people to offer their services as coaches and rotating the coach service throughout the organization.
- Arrange specific training for teams or projects or groups.

- Arrange space so people have enough room to work. That work might be code review, test review, or a lab.

In addition, managers remove impediments or challenges the team can't solve on its own. Consider these scenarios:

- If the team uses ancient machines to build and smoke test, you might need to advocate for faster machines that mimic customer configurations.
- If the team doesn't have all the people they need to complete the work, you might need to advocate for more people.
- If the team can't easily communicate because they don't have the licenses or tools, such as cameras for a distributed team, you might need to help buy those things.

Your time is much better spent on arranging space for the team to solve its own problems and for removing impediments the team can't remove. They can handle the code and tests. You handle the management work.

What if you were promoted from within the organization? Consider pairing or mobbing with the team so they learn what you used to do. As a manager, the last thing you need to do is offer technical assistance. Why? You're dealing with management issues.

5.6 Can You Contribute Technically?

Every manager has a tipping point with respect to how many people the manager can manage and still do technical work. The less seasoned you are as a manager, the faster you reach the tipping point.

If you are new to management, you might be able to lead two other people and still contribute. However, as soon as you add a third person to lead and serve, you may find that you only have about half the working hours available to perform technical work. And the more integrated you are with the technical work, the more likely you are to have some sort of an emergency that requires you to do more of the management.

That's because your management time is not totally predictable.

5.7 Where Does Management Time Go?

Your management time will depend on the kind of team you serve.

Long ago, I charted where my management time went. At the time, I managed a *function*, not a cross-functional, self-managing team.

I was busy all day, every day, running around. Figure 5.1 shows an approximation of where I spent my time:

Weekly Management Work	3 people	4 people	5 people	8 people
One-on-ones (minimum): (30 mins/person)	90 minutes/ week= 1.5 hrs	120 mins/week= 2 hrs	150 mins/week= 2.5 hrs	240 mins/week= 4 hrs
Team Meeting for learning or problem solving: 60 mins plus 30 mins prep	1.5 hrs	1.5 hrs	1.5 hrs	1.5 hrs
Spend time with your manager	1 hr	1 hr	1 hr	1 hr
Problem-solving time spent with your peers on behalf of your team: 4 hours/person	12 hours	16 hours	20 hours	24 hours
HR, Finance, other management work (ranges over the year, call it an average of one hour/person/week	3 hrs	4 hrs	5 hrs	8 hrs
Organizational issues	Unpredictable	Unpredictable	Unpredictable	Unpredictable
Committed management time	19 hours	24.5 hrs	30 hrs	38.5 hrs
Best-case remaining management time	21 hours	15.5 hrs	10 hrs	1.5 hrs

Figure 5.1: Management Time with Manager-Led Team

Because the team members were matrixed into projects, I still had one-on-ones with each person each week. I offered feedback and coaching on their work, their team relationships, and their relationships across the organization.

Notice that I could not easily manage as few as eight people when I had to work with them on their projects. I spent way too much time working with them or for them on their projects.

If I wanted to also contribute technically, my management limit was three people. I could contribute a little bit most days to one project when I only managed three people.

Once I started managing four people, however, the balance of my work swung from technical work to management work. You might be able to manage four people and still do considerable technical work. I had too many emergencies.

I was able to offer feedback. I could coach and teach. I was able to create an environment where everyone could solve problems. But I could no longer perform the technical work myself.

If you use an agile approach, you might need to spend a lot less time personally coaching, offering feedback, and serving the individual people. Successful agile teams integrate several key pieces of the work managers used to perform:

- They can both offer and receive feedback about the work and the team's environment.
- They can both offer and receive coaching about their technical and team concerns.
- And because when people coach and offer feedback to each other, they can create a psychologically safe team environment. That safety can help the team take responsibility for their technical excellence.

The manager is no longer the *sole* practitioner of feedback, coaching, and checking on the team. The team checks itself.

If your team is self-managing, you serve the entire team. Your time might look more like Figure 5.2 on page 58.

Self-managing teams need much less one-on-one time with the manager. That's because the team members will offer feedback and coaching to each other. The team solves most of its problems. (See *Create Your Successful Agile Project* [ROT17] for more details.) The people you serve might still prefer 30-minute one-on-ones as opposed to 20-minute one-on-ones. However, you have the time to offer that option.

Weekly Management Work	8 people	10 people	12 people	16 people
One-on-ones (minimum): 10 mins prep 20 mins in the one-on-one Assume most one-on-ones biweekly	4 people *30 mins/week= 2 hrs	5 people *30 mins/week= 2.5 hrs	6 people * 30 mins/week= 3 hrs	8 people * 30 mins/week= 4 hrs
Organize Community of Practice for team-based learning or problem solving	1.5 hrs	1.5 hrs	1.5 hrs	1.5 hrs
Spend time with your manager (or with others) on more strategic issues	1 hr	1 hr	1 hr	1 hr
Peer coordination to see and remove impediments (Large at first, then more consistent)	15 hours	15 hours	15 hours	15 hours
HR, Finance, other management work (ranges over the year, call it an average of one day/week	8 hrs	8 hrs	8 hrs	8 hrs
Organizational issues	Unpredictable	Unpredictable	Unpredictable	Unpredictable
Committed management time	27.5 hrs	28 hrs	28.5 hrs	29 hrs
Best-case remaining management time	12.5 hrs	12 hrs	11.5 hrs	11 hrs

Figure 5.2: Management Time with a Self-Managing Team

Think my time allocations are too high? Track your time for a couple of weeks and see where you spend your time.

When managers create self-managing teams, several wonderful things occur:

- The manager has much more time to work on impediments, change, and product strategy. That work is much more strategic than the tactical day-to-day work. The manager offers much more value than they would by being a part of the team or as a controller/decision-maker.
- Each manager can either learn to serve all the people on a cross-functional team (or several teams) or contribute in another way to the entire organization. When a manager understands the issues of development *and* testing, as an example, managers see the system and can remove impediments.
- The organization needs fewer managers. Too many managers want the title but not the hard work of management. When

organizations need fewer managers, architects can shepherd the business value of the architecture as a social activity. The teams will have the bandwidth to create the tooling they need to go as fast as possible. And the managers can focus on strategic issues and not on the tactics of getting the product out the door.

You might not have experienced serving a self-managing team. In that case, all the work you do to help people offer each other feedback and coaching will free you to perform your management job better.

If you are still organizing code or tests once you've been a manager for more than a month, beware of not doing either the management job or the technical job well. When you hesitate to delegate your previous work, you implicitly tell the team, "I don't trust you to do the technical work." What's more, you're not doing your management job.

Don't let a crisis force you to realize you're doing nothing well.

5.8 But, My Manager Expects Me to Do Both

Ah, now we come to a real problem. There are some second-level managers out there who think it's reasonable for a first-level manager to manage one or two people and fully participate as a technical contributor. That second-level manager might be correct, but that first-level manager is barely a manager.

As soon as that first-level manager manages a third person, the manager's balance must swing from technical work to management. And if everything has been okay up until then, it will take a crisis for the first-level manager to realize that his or her management responsibilities have to come first.

Explain to your manager that you have management responsibilities that are more important than technical work. You trust your team. You can facilitate their problem-solving. You might even be able to contribute to their problem-solving process. But to get down and dirty in the code, tests, requirements, or project management only hurts your team.

If your manager expects you to do both significant technical work and management work, you have a personal project portfolio problem. Track your time for two weeks so you know where you're spending your time. Then take a stance of curiosity and use these ideas to discuss the problem with your manager:

- Which work is most important, my management or technical work?
- What should I stop doing?
- Here are the risks I see . . .

If you're not sure how to track your work or have this conversation, see the series that starts with the post *Visualize Your Work So You Can Say No*[1] to see boards and how you might lead this conversation.

5.9 Frustrated by Management Work?

If you're like many new managers, you might find the management work frustrating, especially if you didn't receive any training. You might want to escape back into the technical work to feel some accomplishment.

Don't use technical work as a crutch to avoid the frustrations of management work.

Instead, look at your role and what you're supposed to do. Do you need to ask for help with the budget, the project portfolio, coaching, or offering feedback? Ask your boss for help. Maybe even ask the people you serve.

> **Do You Have Impostor Syndrome?**
>
> If you are new to a management role or new to a management role *here*, you might feel a bit like a fraud. You might suffer from Impostor Syndrome.

[1] https://www.jrothman.com/mpd/portfolio-management/2017/02/visualize-your-work-so-you-can-say-no/

> You might be tempted to jump back into the technical work because you *know* you can excel at that work. Don't do it.
>
> If you want to be a manager—even if you're not sure you want to remain a manager—learn how to excel as a manager. You can even ask your team to help you avoid choosing technical work over management work.

Here are three options you might consider:

- Learn and practice your management role.
- Bring in a player-coach as a consultant to help your team practice their alternatives for their work. For example, in the agile software community, I can think of at least ten people I would be happy to bring in as player-coaches. They work with teams as technical leaders, not as managers. Over time, they transition their knowledge and responsibility to the team.
- Decide you want to remain a technical person.

These are just three options. You might think of more.

5.10 What If You Love Technical Work?

If you can't keep your hands off of the technical work, then you might decide that being in management is not for you. In that case, discuss what you *do* want with your manager. It's your career. You can change your mind at any time.

Everyone needs time to learn how to do management work. If you don't want to invest the time, that's one thing. If you do want to invest the time to learn to be a great manager, explain to your boss and to your team that you're learning. You need time, feedback, and coaching to learn to manage well.

Beware of thinking you can be an effective player-coach and still do technical work. You might be one of the four or five people I know who can do that. Most of us, however, don't have enough of the right systems in the organization to support our management work.

In the meantime, watch yourself. Don't commit to technical work *first*. Commit to management first. Then consider any technical work. And consider pairing or mobbing with the team so you can offer the benefit of your experience, *and* you can slide in and out of the team's technical work.

5.11 Options to Move from Player-Coach to Manager

If you've decided you want to move from player-coach to management, ask these questions for the people you lead and serve:

1. Have you clarified the purpose of the work to everyone you lead and serve?
2. Have you helped people practice their feedback and coaching skills so they can create a safe environment?
3. What's the smallest experiment you can try, to see what else people need to know? You might need to lead learning sessions so you can delegate work.

In addition, ask these questions for your manager:

1. What outcomes do you want from my team or group? When you focus on outcomes, your manager might do the same.
2. Create your chart of where your management time goes. (See Where Does Management Time Go? on page 56 for an example.)
3. Assess your project portfolio—for you and your team. Are you and your team able to do all that work?

CHAPTER 6

Can You Trust Your Estimation Gut?

Long ago, when I was a young developer at an anonymous company, one of my managers was disappointed with my progress.

"I know how long the work should take. If I was doing the work, it would be done by now," he said and sneered at me.

"Really?" I could have stopped there. I didn't. "If you had done the work right the first time, I wouldn't be in here mucking around with this, trying to fix everything. I pull something here, and something pops out over there. Of course, I've fixed nine defects by now, nine defects I hadn't planned on fixing. Our customers are thrilled because I've released the already-fixed defects. I just haven't released this feature yet. But you would be done. Good to know. I wonder what else I have to clean up?"

Have I told you that I am the Queen of the Career-Limiting Conversation? My boss didn't fire me that week.

It was a complex piece of code. I could have been more politic in my answer. But I was tired of pushing, pulling, and the puzzles. I wanted some straightforward puzzles to solve, not those roundabout problems. And then when he said he knew how long the work should take? That was insulting. As if I was taking my own sweet time with this.

Ha! I was working hard. I was thinking hard.

This management myth is based on the belief that if the work is simple to describe, then it's easy and fast to do. Uh uh. Do not fall for that one. Managers, architects, technical leads—anyone who has done work similar to this—can fall into this trap. This myth exposes several problems:

- Does the manager understand the work as it stands now?
- Does the technical person understand the work now?
- Do each of them agree on what done means for the work?

Having a snarky conversation as I did is not helpful.

Too many managers fall for the myth that because they used to know something about the work, they can estimate the work better than the people doing the work. If you think that way, read on.

6.1 Myth: I Know How Long the Work Should Take

Sally, the project manager, strode confidently into her meeting with John, the CIO. She'd reviewed the roadmap with the product owner and had discussed the risks with the project team. She was sure, based on the first few iterations, that the project was off to a good start. Sure, she knew that projects rarely stayed on course, but this project had a chance of making the dates.

The product owner knew how to work the backlog, the team knew how to finish what they estimated they could complete each iteration, the architect was embedded into the team—this project was cooking! She was happy. As much as she could project into the future—which wasn't far—this project was going well.

"Hi John. What did you want?" Sally said as she sat down in John's visitor chair.

"I want you to cut 20 percent off the date for this project," John replied. He pointed to the final release in the roadmap.

"Well, that's no problem. We're using agile iterations. You won't get the last 20 percent of the iterations, so you won't get the last x percent of the features, but that's okay."

"No, you don't understand. I want it all. Things shouldn't take this long to do."

Sally frowned and said, "I don't understand. What do you mean, 'Things shouldn't take this long to do.' Do you think people are slacking off? Do you think we are not working hard? What problem are you trying to solve?"

John sighed. "When I was a developer on this system, it didn't take two months to add a feature like this," he said as he pointed to the roadmap and to a specific feature. "It shouldn't take that long. In fact, I added something like that back in the day."

Sally almost swallowed her tongue. She didn't want to try to explain that the team had spent almost a week and pulled all of John's code out for just that feature because it didn't work and was unmaintainable.

He continued, "I wrote that code overnight. I know what it takes to write code for this system. It doesn't take two weeks!"

"Back when you started this product, you didn't have the complexity we now have. It was difficult then, but not the way it is now."

John nodded. "Okay." Sally continued. "And, when we write code now, we write unit tests along with the code. In fact, we write the tests first. We find that when we do that, it helps our design."

John interrupted Sally. "Well, it makes everything take too long. Stop doing that."

"No," Sally said.

"What do you mean, 'No.' I'm your boss," John said. "What I say goes."

"Not when you say something that doesn't get you what you really want," said Sally. "Look, what you want is to finish this project faster, so you can start the next project, right?"

"Right," John replied.

"Okay, so you can stop an agile project whenever you want because we always get to done at the end of an iteration," Sally explained. "No problem. We have tests so we know the code works. We have releases on the roadmap, and if you want to release before or after a 'real' release, we can do that, too."

"Exactly," John said.

Sally shook her head. "But my job as an agile project manager is to ensure that the team gets to practice their professionalism. I serve the team. I also serve you, but the way I serve you is by facilitating the team. So, no, I'm not going to help you get something you don't really want. Remember when we tried to make waterfall work, and you used to try to cut 20 percent off the end of every project schedule?"

John leaned back and smiled. "Yes, that worked."

Sally grinned. "Well, it worked for you the first time. But it killed the team. So, I learned what you did. Since I used deliverable-based planning and incremental approaches with rolling-wave planning, I just gave you an estimate that was anywhere from 20-30 percent larger after the first time you cut my schedule by 20 percent. I padded the schedule. I'm not an idiot. I refuse to let the team suffer because you don't know what it really takes anymore for what the code needs."

"You inflated your estimates?" John asked. "How dare you!"

"It worked, didn't it?" Sally said.

"Well, it did," said John. "I liked the releases. But I don't like it when you pull the wool over my eyes."

"Well, that's why we went to agile approaches. You and I both have a lot more transparency. That's why I say you can stop the project at any time."

John thought for a few seconds and then said, "How dare you say I don't know anymore what the code needs!"

"John, when was the last time you really looked in the code? I mean, really looked in the code? You are a CIO. You don't write code for a living. You don't. You don't know what it needs. You cannot possibly estimate what it takes."

He frowned.

Sally continued. "You're looking at a roadmap, not even an estimate, making a judgment about where we will be in six months, and deciding we are taking too long? You're not being rational. So many things can happen on this project."

John shook his head.

Sally continued. "Look, you tell me what you want to have happen, and I will do my best to make it happen. You want to finish this project by a certain date? Great. Make sure you explain to the product owner what features you think are most important. The product owner will work with you. We will work together to deliver the most important features by the date you want. But I will not tell the technical team to stop being professional. That is the quickest way to get a product we cannot ship. And then we cannot go on to the next project."

John leaned back in his chair and crossed his arms. "I still don't like it."

"Well, I'm not sure exactly what I like," Sally said. "But don't tell me you know how long things should take. We are the project team. We know how long things take. You tell us what project you want us to work on. We will. We will work on the features in order from the product owner. We will be professional. We will not gold-plate anything. But don't tell us how long anything should take. We will tell you how long things will take. Okay?"

"I don't like it, but, okay," John said.

6.2 How Long Will the Work Take?

If you are not familiar with a specific piece of work, it always seems as if it should take less time to complete than it does, especially if the work is conceptually easy to explain. It's even worse if a manager has done similar work in the past.

But what managers forget is that when they previously performed that work, the system was less complex. Or, the environment was easier to work in. Or the language was easier to learn. Something was easier.

Too often, in software, the work is a victim of technical debt or cruft. Long ago, we consciously decided to take a shortcut for more rapid feedback. We worked fast, not to meet a deadline but to learn. We owed the product more work—a form of debt.

More often, what I see is technical cruft. We either purposely did insufficient work to meet a deadline, or we didn't maintain clean code or tests. Doc Norton has a wonderful blog post called Technical Debt versus Cruft[1] that explains the difference between debt and cruft.

The longer the manager has been away from the technical work, the less the manager still knows the technical details. And—as we all know—for software, the details matter.

6.3 Do You Still Know What to Do?

The longer managers have managed, the less they remember the details about the work. (See Can You Be Effective as a Player-Coach? on page 49.)

At one point, maybe that manager did know what to do. But the more senior the manager, the less likely that manager still knows how to perform the work.

Do not allow managers who don't know the technical work to influence the project schedule or the technical environment. People who don't perform technical work should not change the project schedule or buy technical tools. It's fine if those people provide a monetary ceiling—fiduciary responsibility makes sense. But making the final decision? That's up to the people who do the work.

The more you allow the manager to influence your work, the worse your work environment may become.

If you're that manager, remember that a clean code and test environment allows a team to proceed as fast as possible. A crufty environment without sufficient test or other infrastructure prevents the team from the maximum possible speed.

6.4 What Does the Manager Want?

If you have a manager who insinuates himself into your work, ask that manager what he wants. Specifically, ask for the business outcomes the manager wants.

[1] http://docondev.com/blog/2010/10/technical-debt-versus-cruft

In this case, John wants this project to be done faster so the next project can be started earlier. The organization had too much pending work in the project portfolio. When the team finished this project, they could move to the next one.

Sometimes, managers want to release earlier, especially if they aren't using an agile approach. In that case, the team might be able to complete what they're doing and move to the next project.

Whatever the case, the project team always has options. Use business outcomes to decide on the option.

It's okay for a manager to want a project to end early. Managers can want anything. It's how they act on those wishes that might be a problem. As long as managers trust in their project teams, and as long as those project teams work to earn trust, both sides can work together.

When a manager insists on overriding estimates or any other judgments about the work, that manager is incongruent. The manager is not considering the person or the context of the work.

6.5 Options for When You Don't Like the Estimate

If you really think you could do the work fas ter, or the work still takes longer than it "should," consider investing some time to investigate what takes so "long." One way is to spend an hour or two with the team mapping their delays. See Unearthing Your Project's Delays[2] to see how to map the team's actions.

If you continue to think people "should" be able to finish faster, something is off between your perception of the team's reality and their experience. Investigate the team's system and help them to visualize their reality. That takes two parts:

- Map *your* cycle time for decisions the team needs, to make sure you're not slowing the team down. See Measure Your Cycle Time on page 137.

[2] https://www.jrothman.com/articles/2018/10/unearthing-your-projects-delays/

- Ask the team to measure their cycle time as a team. I wrote about that extensively in Book 2.

In my experience, the wait times for a manager's and a team's work outweigh the work time, often by at least one order of magnitude. If you want a team to go faster, look for the delays.

You might not be the cause of those delays. However, you might help others make those decisions faster. I encourage you to read Book 2 to see how you might visualize and manage those delays. This myth is about managing your reaction to the team's estimate.

Given all that, what if you feel you're between the proverbial rock and a hard place with this work? What if you think someone could do it faster?

- If you feel under pressure for a specific date, ask the person—or, preferably the team—what they could deliver by that date. That might not be "all" of the work, but it might be enough.
- Make sure no one multitasks. Sometimes, the team doesn't have a specific goal, and they meander between various products and projects. The more anyone multitasks, the less throughout they or the team has.
- Ask the team if they are willing to map the value stream[3] to see the lead time and cycle time. When teams do that, they often discover they spend too much time waiting for people outside the team and each other. They might be willing to collaborate to reduce waiting inside the team.
- Ask for more transparency. Ask where people see risks and how they expect to manage those risks. Maybe you can remove some organizational impediments so they can finish faster.

[3] https://www.jrothman.com/mpd/2019/09/measure-cycle-time-not-velocity/

CHAPTER 7

When Do You Ask, "Are You Done Yet?"

Back when I was a Director of many things at one company, we had an urgent patch to go to a customer. My VP wanted it "yesterday." Well, time only goes in one direction.

I gathered my Continuing Engineering team and explained the pickle we were in. "Everyone wants this patch right away. The customer is truly pissed. I want to know that we have a fix that works. And while you are working on it, I will need to know updates every morning and every afternoon. I will run interference for you as well as I can."

Everyone groaned. They knew what this meant. We had a small company. The corporate management was just down the hall from our offices. Even though I said I would run interference, nothing would prevent the VP of Engineering, the CEO, or the CTO from popping their heads in "to see what's going on." Everyone wanted to make the customer happy, *right now*.

At the time, I didn't know about kanban boards. I knew about spreadsheets and email. We had four full-time people working on this fix, a significant investment of people and time. Because they swarmed and left notes, I also knew what they planned and what they discovered.

They managed themselves. Their offices were close to each other. Every day, about noon or so, they gathered in my office, so I would have the most up-to-date status. It wasn't quite a standup, because some of the work was what we would now call "spikes," short, timeboxed experiments (At first, we had no idea what was causing the problem.)

As we identified the problem, I explained to management *on behalf of the team* how they narrowed down the problem and identified it. Then I explained to management *on behalf of the team* how they were debugging the problem. Then I explained to management *on behalf of the team* how they were testing the fixes they proposed. Then I explained to management how they were packaging the fix they had decided on.

If we'd had a visual board, this might have been easier. I used email. It took close to a month. It was a very difficult fix.

Notice what I did:

- I explained to the team the results I wanted: as quickly as possible, but it had to be right. Right trumped shoddy.
- I explained that I needed information and how often I needed it.
- I ran interference and kept the rest of the management team informed on a daily basis. My goal was no surprises.
- I explained things on behalf of the team so they got the credit. I was doing my management job, not technical work.

We had sufficient transparency with our management. Because they knew where we stood, I could share the interim results with the customer. The customer was not happy during this month, but they were pleased to know we were working on the fix. By the time they got the patch, they were very pleased. It worked.

I did not micromanage these people. I understood their state. There is a big difference.

If I had stood over their shoulders and asked, "Is it done yet?" I suspect I would have had different results.

My team understood that I was doing my management job. I wasn't able to prevent all senior management interference. But I prevented most of it. In return, the team was free to work together to accomplish their goal: a fix that didn't upset the rest of the system and solved this customer's problem.

It's easy to fall into micromanagement. All of us knowledge workers—managers and technical people—excel as problem-solvers. We want to help other people solve their problems.

However, problem-solving as micromanagement inflicts help on other people. The constant direction or status request are not helpful at all. Micromanagement irritates other people, and it prevents them from doing their jobs.

7.1 Myth: It's Fine if I Micromanage

Sharon poked her head into Heath's cubicle. "Hey, Heath, are you done yet with that fix?"

Heath turned around. "Sharon, you asked me that less than an hour ago. I'm not done yet."

"Well, I need to know when you will be done. Oh, and I need to know if you're using the design we discussed."

Heath started to turn red. "*We* didn't discuss any design at all. *You* told me a design to use. Because *you* used that design back in the day, back when you were a developer. So *you* want me to use it now. Are you delegating this fix to me or not? Do *you* want to do it?"

Damon popped up from his cube on the other side of Heath. He tapped Sharon on the shoulder before she could reply. "Sharon, it sounds as if you need information. It also sounds as if Heath needs time to finish that fix. How about I help?"

Sharon looked relieved. So did Heath. "That would be great," she replied. "I have another Ops meeting in fifteen minutes where everyone is going to ask me when the fix will be done. I'd really like to know the answer." She took off down the hall, texting on her phone as she went.

Damon sat down next to Heath. "OK, tell me what's going on. You sound as if you're at the end of your rope."

"I know this is a critical fix. But Sharon won't let me do my job," Heath said. "It's not just this fix; it's anything. She wants to design this fix for me. She's come over here five times this morning, and it's not even noon. OK, she has that meeting, and I know they're going to rake her over the coals. I got that part. But interrupting me isn't going to help. I need time to think."

Damon prodded. "You said it's not just this fix? What do you mean?"

"I've taken over Sharon's subject matter expertise areas, right? I want to share them. I don't want to be the only person who knows them. That's crazy. Every time I ask for help she says things like, 'I didn't need help when I was the developer,' or crazy things like that. This is a big fix. I said I want to pair with another developer or a developer and a tester, too. She told me I didn't need to. How could she possibly know what I need to do? Is she a mind reader now?"

Damon nodded.

"And for my regular work, when we estimate as a team, she's there," Heath continued. "She's not supposed to be there, but our supposed Scrum Master won't kick her out of the room, so she screws up our estimates. You haven't seen this, because you're a tech lead on another team. She tells us our estimates are too big, so she bullies us into making them smaller. But we can't make them smaller. They are what they are. It's crazy."

Damon sighed and nodded.

"Then she tells us how to design. She doesn't know the code anymore. She's in meetings all the time. But she thinks she does. This is really bad. I don't think I can take it anymore. Maybe I'll quit today. That would serve her right."

"Whoa," Damon said. "I can tell you're really frustrated."

Heath sighed and nodded.

"I learned something important last year," Damon said. "Managers are people, too. I suspect Sharon doesn't know what to do in her new role. She hasn't learned how to delegate or what an agile manager does, so she's insinuating herself into the team. Has anyone provided her with feedback?"

"No. We're just putting up with things."

"OK. You folks have to learn how to give Sharon feedback. For now, I'll talk to her. Would you like me to work with you so you have someone to talk with, just on this fix?"

"Yes, please," Heath replied. "This is harder than it looks."

"OK. I'll timebox our work to ten minutes so I have something to say to Sharon. I'll run interference for you and give her a status. Then I'll come back to you, OK?"

7.2 Learn How to Delegate

If you were one of the best technical people and you were promoted to a manager, you may have to learn how to delegate. (See Consider What You Can Delegate on page 40.) If people outside the team clamor for information and you're not sure what to tell them, you might feel the urge to push the current technical staff aside and do it yourself. You might be faster. You might be right. But unless the technical staff ask you for help, that's wrong.

People want to feel accountable for their own work. People need to both succeed and fail on their own. They are adults—treat them that way.

If you explain to people the results you want and the boundaries of what the acceptable deliverables are, people will deliver. And, as in this case, if you explain that you need information in a timely manner, they will deliver that, too.

7.3 Clarify Which Information You Need When

Sometimes managers micromanage when they need information. In that case, it's easier to create an information radiator (some sort of easy-to-access progress indicator) rather than have the manager come running to you every thirty minutes. Or you can work with a buddy so that someone else runs interference for you. This way, you can concentrate on your technical work, and some other manager will receive the information.

Often, a senior manager needs the information. You can ask your immediate manager to provide the cover for you. If that doesn't work, see if a tech lead or someone else who has the manager's respect will work with you. It's worth a shot.

7.4 Offer Feedback to Managers

Managers need feedback to know that they are micromanaging. They might not need to know when they are headed to the Ops meeting, but they need to know.

Damon spent those ten minutes with Heath and then went to debrief Sharon.

Damon said, "Here's where Heath is right now. I'll be working with him for the next hour, so you can be sure we will be making progress. And there's something else I want to discuss with you. Check with me when you return, OK?"

"No problem. Maybe by then, you two will have fixed the problem," Sharon replied.

When Sharon returned from the Ops meeting, she checked with Damon. "OK, I'm ready. Did you two fix the problem?"

"Not yet. Heath has a good handle on it right now. I'm going to work with him later. But I need to talk to you about something else."

"Oh, what's that?" Sharon asked.

"When you ask Heath for status that often and tell him how to design and implement, you're micromanaging him. Are you aware of that?"

"Well, no. I thought I was being a good mentor or coach. I thought that's what good managers did," Sharon said.

"No, good managers offer suggestions—if people want them," Damon said. "You can ask, 'Would you like help?' And if people say, 'No, thanks,' you back off. Believe me, I know how tough this is to take. Even as a tech lead, I want to tell people what to do sometimes. But I can't. I can offer, but I can't make them do things."

Sharon sighed.

"When you were promoted, did anyone ever tell you about delegation?" Damon asked.

"No, no one ever did," Sharon admitted.

"Hmm. Do you ever have one-on-ones with your manager?" Damon asked.

"Oh, no. Steve says he's too busy. I'm winging it," Sharon said.

"That's a problem," Damon said. "If you want, I can tell you what I know. My boss, Joakim, is a great manager. I'm just a tech lead, so I don't do 'management' per se, but I'm in a lot of the same quandaries. If you want, we can meet once a week and I can tell you what I know.

"That sounds great," Sharon said. "Thanks."

7.5 Recognize Your Micromanagement

Sharon thought she could still "do it all." No one can. It's a bad idea and incongruent if you try.

Ask yourself these questions to see if you're micromanaging:

- How many times a day do you check in with people or a team? How many times a week?
- How often do you ask people if they want your opinion or your help?
- How often do you answer for other people?
- How often do you tell people which risks you want them to manage?

Sometimes you answer on behalf of the team for what feels like a good reason. Your managers might want an estimate *now*. It's very tempting to offer an estimate and placate your managers.

Don't do it.

Instead, practice saying something like, "I can ask the team for an estimate today, and I'm sure we can give you one within a couple of days. If that's not fast enough, I will tell them to stop working on whatever they're doing to create the estimate for you." Your managers don't need to micromanage you, either.

Sometimes you have experience with the design or architecture, and you're worried about where the team is headed. If so, explain that you're worried. Explain your concerns: "I'm worried the design won't take into account these potential problems," and list those problems. Then you can add, "Is there a time you can explain to me how you're addressing those questions?" Wait for the team to explain. Extend the trust the team deserves.

7.6 Options to Stop Micromanagement

Micromanagement causes problems for everyone. It feels as if the manager doesn't trust the person who's being micromanaged. The micromanager might not feel good about always asking or inflicting help. That incongruence is about not extending trust to the people doing the work.

If you don't want to micromanage, consider these options:

- Create information radiators so you don't have to ask anyone about the status. Explain the information you need and how often you need the team to update that information.
- Ask for the results you want, not the process or the method.
- Ask to see visual progress of work, such as demos or prototypes. When people and teams demo their work, you can trust that they are making progress.
- Help people know what "done" means.
- Clarify the risks you see so people can address those risks.
- Extend trust.

When people say no, they don't want your advice, opinion, or help, know that you have helped them achieve independence and knowledge. They are not rejecting *you* as a human or manager. They don't need you for that part of the problem.

See if you can learn to rejoice in their independence. When they no longer need you for everything, you free yourself to do more, and you've created more capacity in your team.

That might feel scary, too. That's okay. If you never feel as if you're working out of your comfort zone, you're probably micromanaging.

Managers need to learn and help the team or group learn. Micromanagement is incongruent with a learning organization. Help yourself move out of your comfort zone day by day.

CHAPTER 8

Does the Team Need Motivation?

I once worked for a manager who ignored all the problems we had. His mantra was, "Let's go, gang, we can do it!" Although I am an optimist, I don't believe in false optimism.

Instead, everyone needs a firm grip on reality. In projects, reality shows up eventually and hits you over the head with a two-by-four.

Reality hits you over the head in corporate management, too. When you ignore problems, bad things occur:

- You invest and continue to invest in the wrong (or wrong-for-now) projects.
- You don't manage the project portfolio at all, and everyone multitasks, not finishing anything.
- You don't realize that the projects aren't going to save themselves. They need some sort of intervention.
- You might not hire the right people when you need them.

Make any of these mistakes often enough, and your revenue and income start a downward spiral. You have to lay people off or take some other drastic action.

Managers don't need to micromanage the actual work. Managers need to manage the *environment* so people can finish work. It's even more necessary for managers to notice and solve problems in the environment.

Encouraging managers can be helpful, assuming you ensure people have the tools and information needed to do their jobs. Cheerleading managers? Not so much. If you are not sure whether you are encouraging or cheerleading, ask the people you serve. They will tell you if your cheerleading feels false or feels like empathy.

That request means you need courage. You might need to offer more transparency to the people you lead and serve. And your manager might not value that transparency.

However, what have you got to lose? I see these choices:

- You lose the respect of the people you lead and serve because you ignore reality with cheerleading.
- You gain respect and trust—and maybe a safer environment—because you acknowledge your reality.

I choose increasing respect every time. The more respect you create in the organization, the more people will help you solve problems. Those problems might be a time-critical product release, salvaging a customer relationship, or creating a new product and service.

People and teams need their managers to have the courage to hear bad news and act on it.

8.1 Myth: The Team Needs a Cheerleader!

"We have another mandatory all-hands meeting this afternoon. I'm going to have a stomachache then," David said.

"What do you mean?" Jenny, his manager, asked. "You haven't even had lunch yet. How do you know? What are you talking about?"

"Look, you know what our wonderful division head, Martin, is going to say. He's not going to take questions about revenue, which is all I want to know about. Then he's going to tell us everything is fine. Well, that's a crock. Everything is not fine."

Jenny nodded. "Yup, he will. And we're not."

"I want to know what he and all the other division heads are doing about the fact that we're losing money. I want to know about the crazy leases we have on all these buildings. Does he think we don't read the financial statements or that we're stupid?"

Jenny shrugged.

"I don't want a cheerleader for a senior manager. I want someone who will give me straight talk. I don't care that it's an all-hands meeting. If you can't tell me that Martin is going to be straight with me, I'm not going."

Jenny sighed and said, "David, I know what you mean. Let me talk to Martin and get back to you. Don't get a stomach ache just yet."

Jenny called Martin and said, "We need to talk before the all-hands meeting. Please, you have to fit me in. This is important. I need fifteen minutes of one-on-one time." Martin agreed, and they decided to have lunch together in Martin's office.

As they unwrapped their sandwiches, Jenny started. "Martin, you and I have discussed this 'cheerleading' business before. Well, I have one more data point. You know David, the technical lead on the SeriousDelivery project? At 9 A.M. this morning, he told me he was going to get a stomachache. He'd planned that because he could not take another all-hands meeting where you played cheerleader instead of explaining how we are working ourselves out of the hole we are in."

Martin's mouth was full, so he held up a finger to tell Jenny to wait.

She shook her head. "No, it's time to be honest and open with our employees. They are adults. We entrust them with our products, our customers, and our trade secrets. What are we waiting for? Tell them the truth. Ask them for help. They will help us."

"Jenny, you and I have talked about this until we were both blue in the face," Martin said. "You're wrong. I know better. People need motivation to keep working when things are not going well."

"Martin, what have you seen or heard that has led you to that conclusion?"

"What do you mean?"

"Just what I asked. People work hard. They sneer at your cheerleading behind your back, and they are still working hard. So, what about this business of motivation do you think they *need* in an all-hands meeting?"

Martin sat back, chewing. He started to open his mouth.

"No, let me finish," Jenny said. "The other managers and I meet with people in our one-on-ones. People have internal motivation. They want to help. They want information and answers from you. Please don't cheerlead. Please reconsider. I'm concerned that more of my team will develop stomachaches. Worse than that, I'm afraid they will leave. And then, where will we be?"

8.2 Intrinsic Motivation Is What Counts

You might think that people need motivation of some sort to do a good job. They don't.

Edward Deci disproved the idea of external motivation back in 1971 in his landmark paper, "*Effects of Externally Mediated Rewards on Intrinsic Motivation*," [DEC71]. Here's a quote I found telling:

> *"Money may work to 'buy off' one's intrinsic motivation for an activity. And this decreased motivation appears . . . to be more than just a temporary phenomenon."*

We might be able to "incent" people with extra money over a short time period. I once worked for an organization that paid the developers extra for a three-month period to stay while the company wound down the product the developers worked on.

For the first four weeks, everything was fine. However, by week six, when the company was not successful in transitioning the customers off the product, the developers started to look for new jobs. The developers knew their jobs were not going to become more challenging. By week eight, all the developers had either given notice or left. Money—even a significant amount extra—was not sufficient to maintain their interest.

That means we can "incent" people with money over a short time period. That incentive does not work over the long term.

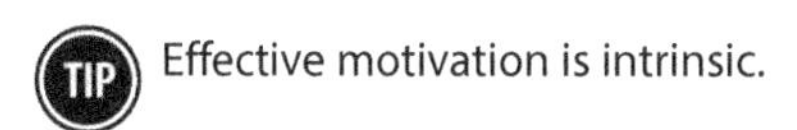

Monetary incentives are different from fair pay for a job. People expect a fair wage for their work.

So, if extrinsic motivation doesn't work, what does work? According to Dan Pink in *Drive: The Surprising Truth About What Motivates Us* [PIN11] the three components of internal motivation are autonomy, mastery, and purpose. Simon Sinek in *Start with Why: How Great Leaders Inspire Everyone to Take Action* [SIN09], says we need to know the why behind the work. That's the purpose.

If people believe in the purpose, and have sufficient autonomy and opportunities for mastery, they will have all the motivation they need.

If you have control over your time at work, then you have autonomy. If you have the chance to improve your skills at work, then you have the chance to master your work. And if you know what the goal or the vision is, then you know your purpose.

External motivation is incongruent. It says to people, "We don't believe you would do a good job on your own. We think you need carrots or sticks to do the work."

8.3 Use Purpose to Solve Problems

When you cheerlead, you deny people the purpose. And if you work for a cheerleading manager, then you don't have the chance to share in the purpose.

The purpose frames the problem for the work. That problem helps the team understand its common goal. A common goal brings a team together. Sharing the purpose is what will help you solve problems, especially if the organization is in trouble.

In this case, imagine if Martin was brave enough to share the organization's problems and said, "We believe in the need for

SeriousDelivery product more than ever. It has the potential to change the world. Our beta customers love it. And we need more revenue to continue to pay everyone. As an organization, we need more revenue to continue to invest in SeriousDelivery. We've already taken management pay cuts. How can we build our customer base faster and gain more revenue, so we're more stable?"

What do you think the reaction would be?

Long ago, I worked in an organization with precisely this problem. When my manager explained the problem, I said, "Sign me up. Let's ship a great product on time, so our customers are happy and tell other people."

Other people might find more meaning in mastery or autonomy. You could phrase this as a mastery problem: "Do you see how we can release smaller chunks of value more often to gain revenue faster?"

If you frame this as an autonomy problem: "As a management team, we don't care how you work as long as you don't create crufty code or tests. We still need to release the product as fast as we can. However, we won't tell you how to work. As a team, can you imagine ways we could release more chunks faster?"

Martin's problem is an example where the technical teams could participate and help the organization. But if the cheerleading manager doesn't share the problem, then how can the team help solve the problem?

8.4 Transparency Helps Everyone

When you have transparency during the good times, everyone shares in the excitement and celebrations. But businesses, just like our lives, have difficult periods.

Managers can share not just the challenges, but share the purpose at all levels, and explain the overarching goal. When managers share reality, people are more likely to want to help the organization succeed.

Cheerleading ignores reality.

In addition, I find cheerleading demeaning and infantilizing. I'm not fond of a parental or paternal approach to management. I might not be the same as everyone in your organization. And in my experience, people at work more often want to be treated as responsible adults.

Do the managers in your organization ever refer to the people you serve as "kids" or part of a "work-family?" Do the managers feel as if they must never be infallible and to make all decisions for the people they serve? If so, you might work in a paternalistic culture. For more information, see "Paternalistic Leadership: A Review and Agenda for Future Research," [PEL08].

Your employees are adults. They are responsible enough to feed, clothe, and shelter themselves. They enter into long-term legal and financial contracts and responsibilities, such as mortgages, marriages, and children. They use prodigious problem-solving skills in their personal lives.

The more innovation your organization needs, the less parental you can be. If people don't know what the problems are, they can't help solve them.

When you use cheerleading as a management "tool," you deny that your employees have the intellectual reason and the problem-solving ability to see what is going on.

8.5 Cheerleading Denies Everyone Courage

If you've been a cheerleader in the past, you will need courage—and possibly vulnerability—to be transparent and admit that there is a problem. If you remain a cheerleading manager, then you attempt to hide the problems. But that's an incongruent stance, and sooner or later, the truth emerges.

It takes courage to be a manager who says, "Here's where we are." If you have been a cheerleading manager, start with that. You might or might not ask the next part: "Will you help me solve this problem?"

You might be surprised by the solutions your staff will offer. At the very least, you will discover that you feel lighter by sharing the burden. And perhaps no one will fake stomachaches at your all-hands meetings.

8.6 Options to Encourage and Create Real Motivation

You might feel as if you *must* cheerlead—especially if your manager does. Instead, consider these ideas to start with creating encouragement and real motivation:

1. Share the truth of the organization. If you feel you can't share bad news, reexamine your assumptions. People often rise to a challenge.
2. Explain the problems you see. You might only see a part of the whole.
3. Clarify the purpose of the team's work. Explain how that purpose reflects the organization's overarching goals.

Extend empathy to the people you lead and serve. You might be surprised by how they respond.

CHAPTER 9

Are You Allowed to Make Mistakes?

I've met too many managers who felt as if they had to be perfect. They couldn't ask for help. They couldn't make mistakes. For some reason, they think never admitting a mistake makes them look "strong" or some such nonsense.

We are human. We all make mistakes. Some of us make multiple mistakes a day. I wish I didn't make mistakes. I do. A funny thing about mistakes: the more I admit them, the easier it is to sidestep *that* mistake again.

When you can't admit that you make mistakes, you make it much more difficult for other people to do so. That means you'll hear bad news very late—too late to do anything about it.

Let me tell you about one of my very worst Bad-Manager Days.

9.1 My Very Bad-Manager Day

My six-month-old daughter had had one of *those* nights where neither of us really slept.

Because it was raining, the babysitter was late. That meant I was late to leave the house. I left the house wearing a blouse stained with baby spit-up. Did I feel like a professional? No. Was I out of sorts? Oh, yes.

I managed to get to my 8:30 A.M. meeting and almost broke my arm patting myself on the back. Afterward, I made my physical rounds and realized one of the support guys wasn't there yet. That was a problem because it was his day to be available to the European sites.

He arrived almost an hour late, dripping wet. "Sorry, I'm late," he said. "The baby was up all night. My wife had to leave early this morning. I'm totally wiped out. I stayed home to pull myself together."

Was I reasonable? Was I understanding? No. I was an ass. (See *The No Asshole Rule: Building a Civilized Workplace and Surviving One That Isn't*, [SUT07].) I said, "We need you here, when it's your turn to be here. Now, leave your emotions at the door."

Luckily, he was smarter than I was. He said, "That's like leaving an arm or a leg. Which one of those would you like me to leave at home today?"

I blinked. Oops. I was having a Bad-Manager Day. I blinked again. I'd better apologize.

I said, "That was one of the more stupid things I said. I apologize. Let me try this again. I realize you've got a lot of stuff going on at home. How can we make things work so you get here on time? You have commitments to other people here."

He said, "Gee, JR, I think you must have lots of things going on at home, too." We both started laughing like hyenas. Yes, we both had children under two, and yes, it was difficult to have predictability in our morning schedules.

It doesn't take much to create a Bad-Manager Day. The car dies, or you get a flat on the way to work. The road has a detour. Your boss wants to change the order of the projects. You were going down the agile path, now you have a new boss who only knows and loves waterfall.

Something changes, whether it's big or small, and boom, it's just enough to cause a Bad-Manager Day. We react in ways that don't make sense.

Maybe it's not even a change that creates a mistake. Maybe you just have a bad day. You got up on the wrong side of the bed. You got angry—maybe even for a great reason—and yelled at someone. The being angry part is fine. Everyone gets angry. It's the blaming, the unreasonable reaction, that's the problem.

Managers are people. And people pay attention to every management action or reaction. In effect, your position magnifies your actions. That means it's even more important for a manager to admit his or her mistakes. Fast. Pronto.

Never let mistakes fester. Think you can gloss over a mistake? Don't even try. The truth always comes out. You can try to forget about mistakes or gloss over them, but those small errors often become larger or rebound on you. I prefer small mistakes I can fix.

9.2 Myth: I Must Never Admit My Mistakes

Robert, a development director, moaned as he plunked himself down in his VP's office. "Juliet, I really screwed up big time. What am I going to do?" He paused. "I can tell you, but I can't admit it to my people. They will never respect me again." He paused again. "I can only tell you because you're coaching me and you told me to tell you." Robert put his head in his hands and moaned again.

Juliet frowned. "If they discover what you did—and they will—they will never forgive you if you don't tell them yourself. What did you do?"

"I yelled at someone in a meeting."

Juliet's eyebrows both shot up. "You what?"

Robert cringed. "I yelled at someone in a meeting. I know, we don't do that here. But I did. I've been having trouble at home. One of the kids has the flu, and I haven't been sleeping. My mother needs to go into assisted living, and my sister is in denial. I'm frustrated. I thought I was handling things, but when Chandra missed her deliverables again, I yelled at her in the standup."

Juliet frowned. "Two questions," she said. "What were you doing in the standup? And why do people have separate deliverables? Why aren't they working together?"

"I want the project to finish."

"So you were at the standup? You can't look at the charts and have a private conversation with the project manager?"

"No. We need this team to finish. We have other projects in the queue and with Chandra not finishing her work . . ."

Juliet leaned forward. "Hold on. Are you the manager or the project manager?"

"I'm the manager." Robert sighed.

"What's your job?"

"My job is to create the environment in which the team can do its best work."

"Can the team members do their best work with you yelling at one of them?"

"No."

Juliet looked at Robert. He sank back in the chair.

"You know, *I* did not pressure you for more work. I don't know where you're getting this pressure from. We need to talk about that. But, first, let's talk about the team. What can you do about the team?"

"I can wait until it blows over?" Robert looked hopeful.

"No," Juliet said and shook her head. "Absolutely not. The longer you wait, the more it will fester. Managers can have a Bad-Manager Day. But you can't let your Bad-Manager Day create a bad environment for the team. And if you want the project finished, you need to talk to the product owner, not just the technical team. Now, you need to acknowledge your behavior and apologize. You need to explain to the team members the results you want and get out of their hair."

Robert looked miserable. "I don't know how to do that."

Juliet smiled gently. "You can say something like this, 'I had a Bad-Manager Day today. I yelled at you. I was upset about other things, and I took it out on you. I was wrong. I should not have done that. I'm sorry.'"

"OK, can we practice this? I feel terrible."

Juliet smiled, and said, "Sure, as many times as you like. As long as you apologize today."

9.3 Managers Make Mistakes

Managers are people, too. They have Bad-Manager Days. And even on good-manager days, they can show doubt, weakness, and uncertainty. They are vulnerable. Managers are not omnipotent.

When we admit we make mistakes, we are congruent. If we ignore mistakes, we blame other people for noticing. That incongruence erodes trust across the organization. Your manager might not trust you. The people you serve certainly won't trust you.

That's why it's critical for a manager to admit a mistake immediately. Sometimes it's difficult for managers to see a mistake when they make one. In that case, acknowledge the mistake as quickly as you can when you realize you have made a mistake. That's because your mistakes—and not admitting them—can cause bigger problems.

9.4 A Manager's Mistakes Cascade

You might have seen cascading defects in a software program. One problem causes another, which causes another, and so on. You fix one defect, and it either uncovers more problems or the fix unmasks more problems. It takes time to bring the system to a reasonable state.

When a manager makes a mistake, it's a similar problem. A manager's mistake, such as Robert's mistake above, can cause distrust in the team. With distrust, people are less likely to want to work or to work together. If there is enough distrust, people look for another job. I bet you've seen entire teams of people leave because of one manager. Or, worse, I bet you've seen the great people leave and the not-so-competent people stay.

9.5 Managers Can Rebuild Trust

If a manager addresses mistakes immediately, without letting those mistakes fester, the manager catches those mistakes and starts to rebuild the trust between themselves and the employees.

If you don't make too many mistakes, people trust you. Your reputation is on your side as a manager. But, if you make management mistakes often, people don't give you the benefit of the doubt. It's difficult to recover once you start to have a reputation as a person who yells or manipulates people.

A weak manager is one who is untrustworthy for a variety of reasons. People trust strong managers. They don't trust weak managers.

Strong managers admit their mistakes. They have the self-esteem to do so. Weak managers paper over the mistake, or they attempt to blame other people. Worse, they may ignore the mistake.

9.6 Wrong Decisions Happen

Management is full of tricky decision making. You can't always tell whether your decision will be right or wrong, but you still have to make the decision.

This is where finding your congruence, as well as trusting yourself, enters the picture. How can you make decisions that balance your needs, the needs of other people, and the context?

Sometimes, managers think that if they don't make a decision, they will be seen as a strong manager because they waited for "all" the data. But managers almost never have all the data. Not making a decision *is* a decision.

Managers have to weigh the risks of waiting for the data against the risks of making the decision now. And, they have to stay emotionally balanced while doing it. If you wait too long, people will see you as a weak manager. Make the decision too early, and you've cut off options you might have used.

You can learn to trust yourself, or say to people, "Here's where I think we need to go, at this time, with the information I have." Your decision might be:

- A small, safe-to-fail experiment based on a hypothesis.
- A time-bound decision, for now: "We'll proceed this way for a month and re-evaluate."
- A money-bound decision: "We'll limit the money we spend to this amount and re-evaluate."

In effect, you're using the ideas in Identify Your Delegation Boundaries on page 44 on *your* decisions.

Like I said, management is full of tricky decision making.

9.7 Ask for Help

What can you do as a manager to build trust, make better decisions, be a strong manager, and not feel as if you have to do your job alone? Ask for help.

Sharing your management pressure can help alleviate it. Robert could have explained his problem like this: "I'm feeling under pressure today. Dave has asked me to make sure we release this product on time, so we can start his project. I know I'm not the product owner. I know I'm not the project portfolio manager. But I'm feeling the pressure. Can you help me here, team?"

Team members might have responded in any number of ways. They might have told him to see the product owner or the project portfolio management team. The coach or Scrum Master or agile project manager might have taken him aside and explained where they were headed. Or, if it was defined at the beginning of the project, one of the team members might have explained the situation. But Robert never gave the team a chance to help him solve his problem.

Remember, you are human, which means you need to admit your mistakes—right away. Your job as a manager is to provide an environment in which the team can do its best work. In return, the team can help you do your best work.

9.8 Options to Make Safe Mistakes

If your organization doesn't encourage asking for help or admitting mistakes, you have a bigger problem. A culture that doesn't allow transparency of mistakes can't learn from those mistakes. That culture becomes a blaming culture. For more information about a blaming culture, see "Beyond Blaming: Congruence in Large System Development Projects" in *PSL Reader*, [MCW96].

Even in a blaming environment, some teams or workgroups can create a culture that works for them. These options might work:

- Be transparent about your concerns. You might say, "I'm worried you can't finish by this date. I see a ton of work in the near future. How worried are any of you?"
- Be transparent about the pressures you feel. You might say, "I was in a meeting with Very Important Customer. I'm supposed to offer status on this project or fix. What is safe for me to say?"
- Be transparent when you need help. "I'm not sure how to create the project portfolio for our group. I would like 20 minutes on Thursday morning."

Not all managers have Bad-Manager Days because of external work pressure. Both Robert and I had Bad-Manager Days from events outside of work. In that case, explain yourself and ask for help. You might say, "I feel as if I'm under a lot of pressure from my personal life. I'm trying to not let it bleed over into my work, but I suspect I am. Please tell me if you think my reactions seem strange to you."

I've suggested you ask for help several times here. When you ask for help, you admit that you are strong and vulnerable. Unless you're a jerk, people respond well to that show of strength.

You don't have to show people you're infallible. You can have a bad-manager day and recover from it.

CHAPTER 10

When Do You Take Time to Think?

As far as I can tell, all managers share these problems:

- You have several hours of meetings each day.
- Your emails are never-ending.
- You have too many texts and other messages.

You have a ton of incoming data. You have many interrupts. You don't have a lot of time to think.

You make decisions without sufficient data—which is a good thing. Remember, Wrong Decisions Happen on page 94. The more you practice making small, safe-to-fail decisions based on a hypothesis, the more you practice making smaller decisions you can change. That frequent small decision-making will help you create more time to think. That's because you don't have to make big decisions too often.

My question for you is this: Do you have access to the data that's easily available? You might need to Create a Structured Meeting on page 103 so everyone can see and hear the same data.

10.1 Myth: I Can Concentrate on the Run

Janet tried to catch Bill, the CIO, on his way to his next meeting. "I need ten minutes of your time to discuss this client problem."

"Good, we'll do a standup later."

"No . . . wait . . . nuts, he left."

Janet grumbled to herself. *I don't want a standup. I want a sit-down, so we can think about and solve this problem. Standups are for status and micro-commitments, not for problem-solving.*

A couple of days later, Janet poked her head into Bill's office. He was standing at the whiteboard with a couple of senior developers.

"Bill, I have a question for you. I can come back later, though."

"No, it's OK." He walked over to the door.

"Look, Bill, this is important. It's an intricate client problem, and I don't feel comfortable discussing it in front of other people. I want some private time with you." Janet frowned. "When do you have time to discuss this with me? I asked you about this problem a couple of days ago. It's not just a technical problem. The client is making funny noises now; it's a client make-nice issue."

Bill shrugged. "OK, we can talk about it in fifteen minutes. I'll be done then."

Fifteen minutes later, Bill was still standing at the whiteboard with the developers.

Janet poked her head in the door. "Bill, remember our discussion?"

"Oh, yes, now I remember. Give me another minute."

Bill took another ten minutes to extricate himself from the other discussion. Once he and Janet started discussing the client issue, Bill asked, "Why didn't you tell me about this earlier?"

"I tried to. You told me we would do a standup 'later.' I didn't want a standup with you. I've been fighting to get time on your calendar. You're always running from one meeting to another. You're not responding to my emails or messages. You just postponed me today, half an hour ago, remember?"

"OK, I get it. Let's solve this problem and go forward."

They did.

Later that week, Bill ran down the hall as Janet made her way to the ladies' room. "Janet, I need to know if your teams can commit to this program."

"I'll tell you later when I've looked at it and seen what it is. I'm on my way to the ladies' room right now."

"I can't wait for an answer."

"Well, you're going to have to. I have to answer the call of nature." She entered the ladies' room.

He stood there with his mouth open for a few seconds. Then, he leaned forward. "Janet?" Bill bellowed through the closed door. "What if I told you the specs now?"

Lauren, the sales VP, tapped Bill on the shoulder. "Excuse me, Bill, I need to get into the ladies' room. Why are you yelling at Janet?"

"I need to know by 5 P.M. if these teams can commit to this program."

"It's 4:45 P.M. now. Why did you wait so long to ask?"

Bill growled, "I just discovered I needed to know."

"Well, that's no good," Lauren said.

"You're telling me? I discover fifteen minutes before an Ops meeting—and why do we have an Ops meeting at 5 P.M. anyway?—that I have to know about this must-save-the-company program, and my program manager is in the bathroom! I need an estimate. They'll have my head if I go in there with no information," Bill said.

"If you just discovered this program, why can't you explain that you'll have the information tomorrow?" Lauren asked.

"Because the Ops committee wants to make a decision today. They only do their standups at 5 P.M. on Tuesdays, and here it is, almost 5 P.M. on Tuesday."

Lauren thought for a few seconds. "You know, standups aren't for decision making."

Janet emerged from the restroom. "That's what I tried to tell you earlier this week, Bill. You're allowed to sit down and have divergent discussions and then come to convergent decisions. Standups are for micro-commitments to each other. Not for decisions about projects and programs."

Bill said, "But—"

"No buts!" Janet said. "I'm your program manager and this is a strategic issue if this really is the next program to save the company.

You need to devote time and energy to solving this problem with me. And, I need to talk with the teams."

"That will take too long—" Bill said.

Janet held up her hand. "Stop right there," she said. "The last time you said we needed a fast commitment, we didn't understand the issues. I had to hire contractors. I thought I had the ability to do so, but you said, and I quote, 'You don't have the authority to commit money on behalf of the organization.' You then told me I need to concentrate on the problem." Janet shrugged. "I can't give you an estimate without knowing more. I'm not going to do this just before you have a meeting."

"But I need to know now," Bill said.

Janet rolled her eyes. "I could be snarky and tell you I had to wait two days to solve that customer problem before."

Bill shuffled his feet. "Yeah, I guess I deserve that." He paused. "But I really do need to know the estimate for this program."

"Okay," Janet said. "Here's one estimate: We can ship something by Christmas. That gives us four months. I know our teams. They love to work on the most valuable thing. They're good at shipping something small. I know we can ship something by then. I don't know what it is or who it's for, but we can ship something."

Bill looked at her, eyebrows up to his hairline. "Have you lost your mind?" he asked.

"Nope," she said. "But you can't possibly give me," she glanced at her watch, "five minutes to think about this and get back to you. I refuse to make decisions that require thought when I'm standing up or on the run. I need to concentrate and think this problem through. And I'm sure I need the teams to decide what the real estimate is."

"Oh boy," Bill said. "I knew those words about concentration would come back to bite me. OK, let me have it. What do you suggest?"

"Let's have a revolution and tell the Ops committee how to make decisions!" Janet said.

Lauren laughed, "Well, I like the revolution part, but maybe we won't tell them. Maybe we can sell them."

Janet and Bill both laughed at that.

"OK," Bill said. "Let's explain what standups are for and why they aren't for major decisions. After that, you and I will get together and discuss the problems they want this program to solve."

"Tomorrow," Janet said. "When you and I can make time to concentrate."

10.2 When Do You Make Time to Concentrate?

I see many managers attempt to make decisions while they run from one meeting to another. I also see managers make decisions when they stand up. Now, there is nothing wrong with standing or walking. I'm a big fan of walking to clear your head or walking with a colleague to discuss a problem.

The problem I see is when people throw problems at you—often several problems simultaneously—and you try to solve them without concentrating or focusing on any of them.

If you aren't able to separate the problems from one another—or even properly learn about each problem—you can't solve them.

In this story, Bill was incongruent in several ways:

- He didn't manage his actions well and placated Janet about the time he would have to work on problems with her.
- He blamed Janet for not offering an estimate when she didn't have an opportunity to think.
- He was all set to placate the Ops committee and offer a solution to a problem no one had truly considered.

Bill was all set to become an obstacle.

Managers provide the most value to the organization when they use their position to remove obstacles for other people. That means solving problems. It also means that you have to pay attention to what problems you solve and how you solve them.

10.3 When Do You Decide?

I see many managers try to decide quickly. Some decisions even benefit from quick decisions while standing up. Where to have lunch is one of those decisions; especially if people decide just before lunch!

But, if you are trying to decide on the value of projects or interview candidates or provide feedback to people—unless you are walking with someone, consider creating an environment that allows you to concentrate.

For me, the environment for concentration includes:

- An agenda so we know what we want to discuss.
- An environment that fosters discussion. This might be a conference room. It might be some other location.
- We have all the people we need.

I've seen these environments: meeting rooms with whiteboards, a walk if it's just two people, or across a visitor's table in someone's office. You need to be able to see the problem statement and the related data. As long as you can do that, you're OK.

10.4 How Do You Concentrate?

Everyone concentrates differently. Maybe you pace while you concentrate. You are standing up, walking. In that case, have an agenda of the problem on the whiteboard.

Maybe you lean back in a chair and put your feet up. Maybe you lean forward and make notes. Maybe you doodle.

Here's what I do know about concentrating: You are not concentrating if you're looking at your phone—unless, of course, you have the data about the problem on your phone. You might not concentrate if you're looking at any other electronic device.

Don't think you can multitask and devote enough attention to this problem. You can't.

Focus on the problem at hand. I suspect that some management teams adopted the standup so they would stop looking at their cell phones. That might have worked to solve the how-do-people-focus problem, but it doesn't work for a serious, in-depth discussion. Is there another way?

10.5 Create a Structured Meeting

You can create a meeting that is limited to one hour or less. On the agenda, create segments that are timeboxes, each not longer than ten minutes. If you are discussing a thorny issue, share the data in advance, so everyone is prepared for the meeting. Then, you might use an agenda like this:

- Problem explanation, including what the data might mean (5 minutes)
- Problem brainstorming (7 minutes)
- Divergent-thinking to generate options (10 minutes)
- Convergent-thinking to select possible options (10 minutes)
- Action item discussion and next steps (5 minutes)

This is a template you might choose to adapt to make it work for you. However, you can try something similar, varying the timing to suit your specific circumstance. The nice thing about timeboxing everything is that people can maintain their focus for the almost thirty minutes this takes. When they realize they are not spending their entire day in a meeting, they are more likely to focus on the problem you want them to solve.

10.6 Sitting Might Not Be the Answer

I agree that sitting in seats is not always the answer. People need to move. Some managers I know are so sleep deprived that they would fall asleep if they sat for more than ten minutes. That's a symptom of yet another problem!

Working together and using your entire body to solve problems is useful. You can do this and still concentrate. Some people like to work at the whiteboard together. That's a form of management problem-solving.

Some people like to brainstorm while writing, instead of speaking. Since many technical managers are from the introverted side of the house, this might work for you. If you have many candidate solutions, form several teams and have the teams evaluate the solutions in parallel, timeboxing their evaluation. Ask them to gather in another meeting to present their findings and discuss the next steps.

Managers solve problems, just as technical teams do. Their problems are different, but the process is similar. Since managers are so accustomed to running from one meeting to another, they might not realize when they need to move into problem-solving mode.

Solve one problem at a time by concentrating on it, and make sure you have actually solved it. Then you can move on to the next one.

If you have a problem, think through solutions, make a decision, and then continue with the rest of your day. You can't solve problems if you are running around, never thinking.

10.7 Options to Make Time to Think

Thinking is work. When you take time to think, you can focus on the problem at hand, solve it, and move to the next issue.

If you don't have enough data, see if there is some step you can take that offers you a little data to make progress on this issue. Then you can reconvene with enough data to make a decision.

Make sure you take the time you need to think. Here are some ideas:

1. Which incoming communications can you batch? For example, I batch my email. I don't allow it to interrupt me every time I receive a new email. I create agreements with teams about when I will respond to which incoming communication.

2. Clarify each meeting's purpose, the people who need to be there, and which data you'll discuss. If the people who create the meeting don't realize the value of this step, discuss the ideas in Measure Your Cycle Time on page 137. Help everyone learn that a little meeting preparation allows managers to speed through their discussions and then decisions.
3. Consider meeting with your colleagues, one-on-one regularly. The more you meet together, the more you all understand systemic problems, such as the problem Janet and Bill struggled with earlier in this chapter.
4. Consider the smallest decision you can make and then adapt later, as you learn more.

CHAPTER 11

Are Problems Bad?

I once worked for a manager who proudly said to me, "Don't bring me a problem without bringing me a solution." I blinked once. Then I asked, "Why would I bring you a problem I could solve?"

He stopped and said, "Ooh." Some of you will recognize that as the programmer's refrain. "Oooh," is what you say when you realize the computer has done something you told it to do but not what you meant it to do.

"Don't bring me a problem without bringing me a solution" is an example of management incongruence. In this case, the manager blames the person for not knowing better.

Managers might not realize they are incongruent when they say things like this. The manager might not know better.

My manager wanted to challenge me. Believe me, I was challenged! I wasn't being lazy. I wasn't being stupid. I was stuck. I needed help. I didn't know where to go for help.

Even in agile teams, the manager might not have the answer. But the manager might be the right person to free the impediment, to know who has the answer, or to help with problem-solving.

When managers have rules about problem-solving, they make life difficult for everyone else. Managers don't have to be perfect. They have to work hard at staying congruent, which is different than being perfect.

I like to see problems as possibilities. I might be able to offer help. I might need to ask for help. One of the trickier things about problem-solving is knowing *when* to ask for help.

11.1 Myth: I Must Always Have a Solution to the Problem

Janet, a developer, hesitated before going down the hall to her manager, David's, office. She turned around, sat back down, and sighed. Steve, a fellow developer, stopped by her cubicle and asked, "What's wrong?"

"I have this problem and I need to ask David a question. I'm really stumped. But he's going to tell me, 'Don't bring me a problem without a solution.' Like that's a helpful answer. Why would I go to him if I had a solution?"

Steve asked, "What have you done?"

"I made this matrix of potential solutions, see?" She pointed to a table in her engineering notebook. "I tried these combinations. None of them work. I tried these things. Nothing works. I asked Tranh for help. He's stuck."

"He's stuck? He's the expert!"

Janet sighed. "I know. If he's stuck and I'm stuck, I don't know what we're going to do. I've tried the Rule of Three. We really need help. David is the last one who worked on that code before he became a manager. It's so darn clever, I don't understand it."

"Janet, this is serious. We need to address this problem. This could put the entire release in jeopardy."

"You're telling me? But David is going to give me some stupid remark about how it's my problem now or how I shouldn't bring him a problem without a solution, and then he's going to blame me for his stupid code. If he wasn't so set on being clever back when he was a developer, maybe I could understand his code. But he didn't write any tests. I've been writing unit tests, and I can't get any of them to pass. This is all screwed up."

Steve thought for a minute. "Okay, we need to go meta on this."

"Go meta?"

"Yes, the problem isn't the problem. It's your reaction to the problem."

"Now it's my reaction? You're going to blame me for his code?" Janet was incredulous.

"Okay, hold on a minute," Steve said. "You're being reasonable. But you're ready for David to be unhelpful, and you're stressed and you need help, right?"

"Yes."

"You need help on this problem, right?" Steve asked.

"Yes."

"So, you've tried the standard operating procedure of writing unit tests, and they haven't worked. You've tried experimenting six ways from Sunday, and that hasn't worked. You need other help, such as old-style reviews, right? And we don't have time for that built into the iteration, right?"

"Yeah," Janet said slowly, "I'm beginning to see what you mean. Start providing him some other options and then let him take it from there."

Steve nodded. "Right. He's not stupid or a jerk, but he is kind of defensive about his old code. And, you nailed it when you said he hates it when we don't bring him some alternatives. So, let's think of some."

Janet smiled and said, "I'm really glad you stopped by."

11.2 Manager Rules Prevent Easy Problem-Solving

Some managers have rules about problems. Some managers think they should be able to have an answer to every problem. I'm not sure why managers should feel that way. They can't possibly have an answer to every problem. They haven't read every book. They can't remember every line of code they ever wrote. Even though they may not even have written the code or the test or the requirement, many managers feel as if they should have an answer.

Some managers don't want people to bring them problems if their people are going to be emotional about the problem. They think, "What if Sally yells and screams? What if Bob cries?" Many of us are not comfortable with our employees' human-ness at work. The first time someone cried in my office, I felt scared and uncomfortable and didn't know what to do. I finally said, "I'm sorry you're sad, and I don't know what to do." My employee replied, "Oh, that's ok. I'll be better in a minute or so." I was lucky. But you might be scared of what your employee might say or do.

Some managers don't want people to bring them problems if they can't take action and do something about it. It sure sounds like Janet has one of those wicked problems that requires very different thinking. If David is afraid that he'll look like a fool or appear incompetent, he'll find it harder for him to help resolve Janet's problem. Some of us feel inadequate or incompetent if we don't have a solution for every problem that comes through our door.

Many manager rules belong to the general perfection rule:

I must always do a perfect job.

I have had good results when I transform my rules into guides.

11.3 Transform Your Manager Rules to Guides

I can't eliminate all of my rules. Sometimes, I don't even realize I have a rule. However, once I'm aware of the rule, I've had good results transforming my rules into guides. I learned about this practice in *Becoming a Technical Leader* [WEI16].

This is an example of a rule transformation, using the perfection rule:

1. State the rule precisely: "I *must* always do a perfect job." That's a compulsion.
2. Instead of the compulsion, offer yourself a choice. Change the *must* to *can.* "I *can* always do a perfect job."
3. Change the certainty in the "always" to possibility. "I can *sometimes* do a perfect job."

4. Select three or more circumstances when you can follow this guide now:
   - If I know enough to do that part of the job.
   - If I can enlist others to help me do that job.
   - If the constraints around my work allow me to do the work.

We all have rules that govern our behaviors. Especially as managers, the more we are aware of our rules, the more we can choose to follow those rules. Or, we can create guides that might help us more.

If you don't have a perfection rule, use this example with *your* rule and see how you might offer yourself more possibilities.

David, Janet's boss, was concerned about his appearance of incompetence. He might have transformed his rule in this way:

1. I must *always* appear competent. (The rule statement.)
2. I *can* always appear competent. (Create a choice.)
3. I can *sometimes* appear competent. (Start of the guide).
4. Under these circumstances:
   - When I know enough about the details of the problem.
   - When I can work with others to increase my knowledge.
   - When I have time to devote to this topic.

That rule transformation might help David encourage people to bring him problems, not solutions.

11.4 Rules About Problems Won't Make the Problems Vanish

The problem is that our rules won't make problems vanish. We have to become effective problem-solvers even if we have these rules.

Here are some possible alternatives if you have such rules about problem-solving:

1. Try these words, "Tell me about the problem." Ask your staff to brief you on what they perceive as the problem. Sometimes, people become stuck when they *think* about the problem for too

long. As soon as they articulate it to someone else, they might think of several possibilities. Or, you might think of some.

2. Ask people, "What do you want to have happen?" Sometimes people have too many possible solutions. Even if they can't see a solution, they sometimes see the result they want to achieve.
3. Ask people, "Do you have ideas I should consider?" A person might not have a fully formed solution, but they might have some ideas.
4. Use the Rule of Three in your problem-solving.(See Managers Can Help Unstick Problem-Solving on page 31.) One solution is a trap, two solutions create a dilemma, and three possibilities break logjam thinking, which helps people think of more possibilities.
5. Say to your team, "I don't know what to do. Let's brainstorm with other people. Who should we involve in a solution?"

11.5 Acknowledge Your Feelings

Your feelings about problems won't make them go away. If you acknowledge your feelings, they might not be so overwhelming. Because of this, you might try a proactive approach to problem discovery instead of trying to avoid the problems.

Look for problems early, when they tend to be smaller and easier to fix. Try changing your reaction from "don't bring that to me" to "let's get more information to go forward."

Look for problems when they're small. Small-and-early problems are often easier to fix than large-and-late problems.

While you don't have to know the answers, being an effective and competent manager means that you can facilitate a way to discover the answers.

11.6 Problems Might Be Possibilities

Early in my career, I thought of problems as bad and that *I* needed to generate a solution. I now realize that the more I invite people into my problems, the better ideas I might see, and the faster I might solve the problem.

I now think of problems as opportunities to collaborate with other people on the solution. I don't even have to know which solution is "right" at first. I can create a variety of possibilities to solve this problem.

The more I invite other people into the problem-solving, the more fallible I can be. The more I can experiment. Often, the more I learn.

I don't need all the answers. Neither do you. Not as long as we surround ourselves with capable people.

11.7 Options to Consider Problems as Possibilities

You might not have the "don't bring me a problem, bring me a solution" reaction to problems. However, many managers don't enjoy seeing or hearing about problems.

Consider these options to help you see and solve problems early when they are small:

1. Ask about impediments or obstacles to the work. You might ask, "Is there anything that you're stuck on?" You might not be the one to unwedge the problem. However, you might know who can help.
2. Assess your rules about problems and your role in solving those problems. I don't always realize I have a rule about a problem until I see that rule in action.
3. As you acknowledge your feelings about the rules and problems, see if you can Consider These Principles for Managing Yourself on page 13 to create alternatives.

Problems aren't bad—they offer information that something isn't working right. You can help create an environment where people can solve those problems.

CHAPTER 12

How Much Do You Trust the People You Serve?

We use the word "empowered" a lot in our organizations. I think of trust when I think of empowerment. When we say we empower people, we most often trust people to do a great job. Managers might have to create some boundaries or guidelines for the work. Then, empowered people have an expectation: that no one—regardless of hierarchical title—violates those boundaries.

Long ago, I was a project manager and senior engineer for a company undergoing a Change Transformation. You know the kind, where the culture changes along with the process. The senior managers had bought into the changes. The middle managers were muddling through, implementing the changes as best they could.

The managers didn't change very much. Those of us who worked on the products—we had to change the most. The changes weren't as significant as an agile transformation, but they were big.

One day, the Big Bosses, the CEO, and the VP of Engineering spoke at an all-hands meeting. "You are empowered," they said. No, they didn't say it as a duet. They each said it separately. They had choreographed speeches, with great slideshows, eight-by-ten color glossies, and pictures. They had a vision. They just knew what the future would hold.

I managed to keep my mouth shut.

The company was not doing well. We had too many managers for not enough engineers or contracts. If you could count, you could see that.

At the time, I traveled back and forth to a client in the midwest. I charged my expenses on my personal credit cards and submitted expenses.

At one point, the company owed me four weeks of travel expenses. I asked Accounting for my reimbursement. They said they were pushing reimbursements out for eight weeks.

I quietly explained that no, I was not going to book any more airline travel or hotel nights until I was paid in full for my previous travel. I actually said these words to the head of Accounting: "I'm empowered. I can refuse to get on a plane."

It might have taken all of five minutes for what I said to permeate the organization.

As soon as I returned to my desk, I called my boss to tell him. He laughed for a long time and said it was quite funny. My boss agreed I should be reimbursed before I racked up more charges.

Somehow, they did manage to reimburse me that week. I explained that from now on, I was not going to float the company more than a week's worth of expenses. If they wanted me to travel, I expected to be reimbursed within a week of travel. I would send in my expenses on the Monday after the trip. They could reimburse me four days later, on Friday.

"But that's too fast for us," explained one of the people in Accounting.

"Then I don't have to travel every other week," I explained. "You see, I'm empowered. I'll travel after I get the money for the previous trip. I won't make a new reservation until I receive all the money I spent for all my previous trips. It's fine with me. You'll have to decide how important this project is. It's okay."

The VP came to me and tried to talk me out of it. I didn't budge. I told him that I didn't need to float the company money. I was empowered.

"Do you like that word?"

"Sure do."

"Do you feel empowered?" he asked.

"Not at all. I have no power at all, except over my actions. I have plenty of power over what I choose to do. I am exercising that power. I realized that during your dog-and-pony show."

He managed to keep his poker face. He stayed silent.

"You're not changing our culture," I said. "You're also making it more difficult for me to do my job. That's fine. I'm explaining how I will work."

He shook his head and walked away.

As employees, we trust that the company will respect us: our time, our money, and our work. As managers, we decide how to create that trust. That's part of managing with integrity.

Too many managers talk about empowerment not as how people exercise their agency and autonomy but as a way to make people take more responsibility. That's a form of incongruence, specifically blame. If you don't do what the management desires, they blame you for expecting something different.

When the organization expects people to "stick their necks out" or "take responsibility," they're actually blaming you for not doing what they want. Instead, the managers—the people who explain the policies—need to extend trust.

Otherwise, this empowerment business is a lot of hot air.

12.1 Myth: You're Empowered Because I Said So

"Larry, I need VP approval for this," said Josh, the Director of Engineering.

Larry looked annoyed. "This is only $30. Why am I signing off on $30?"

"Because I have no signature authority on anything. Even though I'm a director, I can't sign off on any discretionary purchases. I have no capital equipment authorization. I have a company credit card for when I travel and interview, which is good, because I do take people out for lunches and dinners. But I have to say, I don't feel much like a director here. I'm not empowered the way I thought I would be when you offered me this job."

Larry stiffened and sat back in his chair. "Is it about the money? I might be able to do something about purchasing power."

"No, the discretionary purchases are just one indication that the company doesn't trust me. Look, empowerment is based on trust. You might trust me, but the company doesn't trust anyone in engineering to do our jobs right."

Larry cocked his head to the side.

"Let me see if I can clarify," Josh said. "We are supposedly agile, right?"

"Uh, yeah."

"We can't get our supposed product owners to work with us in our iterations. And the acceptance test people are just as bad. Our iterations aren't even two weeks. They're really eight weeks. That's four weeks for the product owners to hem and haw about what they think they want in a two-week iteration, two weeks for the developer and QA team to work on it, and another two weeks for the acceptance test people to accept it. That's just nuts."

"It's that bad?" Larry asked.

"Yup," Josh said. "When I talked to the product owners and mapped the flow for them, they told me they were too busy to talk to me, that they would only talk to a VP."

One of Larry's eyebrows went up.

"Likewise when I talked to the acceptance test people. We can't solve problems at our level. I'm not empowered to do anything. I can try, but we are so hierarchical, it's not worth it."

"Wow," said Larry. "I had no idea."

"I didn't think so," Josh said.

"What can I do?"

"Larry, this is a culture problem. You can tell me I'm empowered, but that doesn't mean anything. I can't solve cross-functional problems;

I can only solve problems inside engineering. But our problems span the organization." Josh paused. "You're part of the problem, you know. You keep canceling our one-on-ones. Have you talked to any of your directors in the past month?"

"Uh, no. I've been really busy."

"I'm sure you have been. But if you talk to your directors, I bet each of us has the same story."

Larry looked down and sighed.

"You can't just tell us we're 'empowered.' Empowerment is a cultural thing, and we don't have it here. If you are too busy to talk to us, you can't help us solve problems at our level. Empowerment is just a word. You want it? You have to walk the talk. You have to trust me to solve problems at my level. You have to trust all of us."

"Josh, are you looking for a job elsewhere?"

"What do you think?"

12.2 What Does Empowerment Mean?

When management tells a group of people they are empowered, it means those people have the power to make a set of decisions without their managers second-guessing them. The employees are supposed to take initiative, but in many organizations, it's not clear who is supposed to make decisions about what.

Consider using the word *trust* instead of empowerment.

Empowerment is about trust and delegation. The managers trust the people to see the issues. Management delegates the problem-solving, possibly within certain boundaries, to the people who see the issues. The people decide what to do.

That means that managers cannot blame others if people act in ways the manager doesn't like. See Support Your Team's Decisions on page 41 for more details.

Use congruence as a way to clarify boundaries and trust people.

12.3 Clarify Boundaries

There may be good reasons for boundaries around spending in an organization. But if there are, the accounting or finance departments would gain goodwill and empathy by sharing those reasons with everyone.

Everyone in the organization makes decisions about projects and problems. It doesn't matter if you are in facilities, IT, or engineering, you make decisions that affect the health of the organization. Every. Single. Day.

Empowerment is not just an agile thing. So, it makes sense to understand the boundaries of your decision-making whether you are agile or not. However, the more agile you want to be, the more you want to push decision-making down to the people with the problems. Otherwise, the cost of delay rises as you wait and wait and wait for a decision by the people in charge.

When the decision-making boundaries are not clear to everyone, collaboration across the organization suffers. Some people retreat to safer boundaries, even if that makes the work more difficult for others. They cover their tushes (also known as CYA). These people are afraid to make a mistake.

12.4 Telling Isn't the Same as Being

You can tell people they are empowered until you are blue in the face, but that doesn't change anyone's mind. Only your actions can change their minds.

Here is one way to demonstrate empowerment:

> You can say, "Here are the results we want for the product." (You might ask the team to please provide you with their release criteria.) "However you get there is fine with management. Please provide us demos and status every couple of weeks so we can see your progress along the way. If you need help, please ask us. We want to be involved in that way. However, you have control over how you develop the product."

Notice that you didn't have to say the "E" word. You explained the results you wanted. You explained how you would check in with the team. You said you would be available for help. You also said team members had control over how they developed the product. You set the boundaries and provided the team with enough room to move.

You don't want teams or people to run open-loop; you want them to act responsibly. In my experience, people do their best to act with the best interests of the organization, as long as you tell them the results you want.

It's up to you as a manager to be specific about the results you want, not the process of how to achieve the results. Do that, and you will have empowered people.

12.5 Options to Extend Trust

If you want people to be empowered, you need to trust them.

Consider these ways to extend trust:

- Clarify any boundaries for the work. Do the people need to deliver something by a specific deadline or stay within some sort of regulatory boundaries? Make sure the people know.
- Clarify any decision-making boundaries. Do people have any money constraints? Or do they need to use certain tools to stay within the organization's security boundaries?
- See if you can eliminate any processes that govern the organization. Many organizations have rules about how their employees should and should not act. They have rules about reimbursement, often to the detriment of the employee.

How can you make a more humane organization? That will go a long way toward building trust.

CHAPTER 13

What Does "Indispensable" Mean?

Years ago, I was the expert for two specific products in a small development organization. When it came time for my manager to divide up the work, I always got those products to add features to, or maintain. That was fine for a while until I got bored. I went to my boss with a request for different work.

"Who will do the work if you don't?" My boss was concerned.

"Steve or Dave will. They're good. They can take over for me." I knew my colleagues. They could do the work.

"But, they'll have to learn what you do."

"I know. I can take a few days to explain if you want. I don't think it will take a few days to explain. They're smart. I'm still available if they have questions."

"I don't know. You're indispensable where you are."

I faced my boss and stood up. "No one is indispensable. And, if I am, you should replace me on those systems anyway. What are you going to do if I leave?"

My boss paled, and asked, "Are you planning to leave?"

"I don't know. I'm bored. I want new work. I told you that. I don't see why I can't have new work. You need developers on these projects." I named three of them. "Why do I have to keep doing work on the old stuff when I want to do new things? I don't see why I should. Just because I've been doing it for a year is no reason to pigeon-hole me. No. I want new work. I'm not indispensable. You can hire someone, and I can train that person if you want."

My boss reluctantly agreed to let me stop working on the old systems and work on the new projects. I was no longer indispensable.

The problem with being an indispensable employee is that your options are limited. Your boss wants you to keep doing the same thing you've always done. Maybe you want that, too, for now.

The problem is that one day, you realize no one needs what you do. You have become such an expert that you are quite dispensable. You have the same year of experience for several years.

Instead of being indispensable, consider how to help other people learn your work. What do you want to learn next? You need to plan your career development.

What do you do if you're a manager, and you have indispensable employees? "Fire" them.

I'm serious. When you have people who are indispensable, they are experts. They create bottlenecks and a cost of delay. If you need flexibility in your organization, you need people who know more than one area. You need teams who are adaptable and can learn quickly. A narrow expert is not what you need. (See *Diving for Hidden Treasures: Uncovering the Cost of Delay in Your Project Portfolio* [RE14] for more information about the causes and implications of the cost of delay.)

When I say "fire" people, I mean don't let them work on their area of expertise alone. Create a transition plan and help the expert discover new skills.

Why should you do this? Because if not, other people across the organization may want to reinforce this one person's expertise. Sometimes with quite bad results.

13.1 Myth: You Believe in Indispensable Employees

Two development managers were arguing: "I need Tom on my team," Chase said. "He has the specific knowledge I need. We're not going to be able to release unless we get Tom on my team."

Pierce retorted, "You can't have him. He's working really well with my team. He likes my team. Forget it."

They went back and forth for a couple of minutes.

Sharon, the VP of Engineering interceded. "Can anyone else do that work, Chase?"

"No. Tom worked in that area a couple of years ago. He trained several people, but they all left."

Sharon cleared her throat. "Well, there you have it. Move Tom. He's the only person who can do that work."

"No, that's crazy," Pierce said. "Chase, your team can learn how to do the work if you give them a chance. You haven't even told them what it entails. You just keep promising them they don't have to learn. You keep telling them 'Tom is coming, Tom is coming.' You're preventing them from learning." He paused. "I'll loan Tom to you for a week to help your team learn, but Tom likes this team."

"No. Tell Tom he has to move," Chase said.

Sharon nodded. "Pierce, we need this work done now. Tell Tom he has to move. He's indispensable."

Pierce shook his head. "No. You tell Tom he has to move; I'm not doing it. Both of you are being ridiculous. Are you telling me that if a person develops expertise and becomes 'indispensable,' they get stuck with the same job their entire professional lives here? Forget it." He stood up. "I'm leaving before I say anything else. Don't do this. Please, think about this for more than the two minutes you've spent on it."

Pierce left.

Sharon turned to Chase. "Wait a minute. Let me ask you a couple of questions. Have you really been telling your team that Tom is coming and that they don't have to work on this without him?"

Chase nodded. "It's really intricate code. We don't have the tests to support the work. It would be much faster with Tom."

"Can your team learn how to do this work at some point?" Sharon wanted to make sure they were capable of doing the work.

"Well, I'm not sure. I think so. The problem is that this team is part of the move to another state, and I'm not sure how many people will stay once we move."

"Wait a minute. You want to yank Tom away from a team he likes and his current community?"

Chase had the grace to look sheepish. "Well, yes. But it's for the good of the company."

"No, it isn't. Look, what we do is work, not slavery. If he's this good, how long do you think he'll actually stay here if we do change his team and ask him to move? Worse, we set a precedent for management idiocy. No. Rethink your options. Pierce is right. Do not move Tom. He can't be indispensable to you."

13.2 Indispensable Employees Create Bottlenecks

Indispensable people are bottlenecks in the organization. They prevent other people from learning what the expert knows, people who might like to learn and grow.

I've seen too many "indispensable" employees disrupt everyone else's work. They might be arrogant in how they prevent other people from learning, although that's not the case here. You have people who are stuck in their current roles, unable to learn or grow in any way, because they must be able to serve the organization in their current role.

Every person who acts as a bottleneck delays your projects. That's because work will queue behind this person until he or she can get to it.

That's not good for the person, the team, the project, or for management.

13.3 What Do You Do with Indispensable Employees?

I already said you consider "firing" the indispensable employee. Don't actually fire them, but make sure they are no longer indispensable or bottlenecks in the organization. There is no reason for anyone to be the *one* person that everyone depends on.

> **Are All of Your Employees Bottlenecks?**
>
> I once consulted with an organization where the average longevity was 20 to 25 years. And the average age of the employees was almost 60. I checked with a senior manager. I said, "You'll end up with many indispensable employees who want to retire, all at the same time. Do you want that to happen?"
>
> He said no, he didn't. We started with "retraining" the current staff.
>
> The cross-training had significant side benefits. Some people did retire or choose reduced work time. However, some people postponed retirement altogether. The people who remained felt more energized because they had new challenges.

How can you "fire" an indispensable employee? If you see an employee falling into this role and you have enough time, suggest that your expert does not work alone while you organize a one-week transition plan.

If the indispensable employee works as part of a team, a one-week transition period might be sufficient. However, if the employee works alone or one-on-one with another person, one week might not be enough time to transition all the work. However, one week is enough time to start a handoff of the work to another person or team.

If the team can't learn everything in one week—and don't be surprised if they can't—make sure team members decide how long they need to learn on their own before they call the expert for help. Do they work as a team for three or four hours? Or will it be a day? Have the team and the expert decide together what is reasonable.

Over time, the team should call the expert less often. If after a month or two the team still calls the expert often, the expert can make herself unavailable for longer periods of time. Instead of responding in a day or so, the expert would respond in a couple of days and then perhaps three days. The idea is that the team still has the expert available—but not easily available. The team needs to learn how to work together to solve problems.

13.4 Consider the Growth Mindset

In the growth mindset made famous by Carol Dweck in her book, *Mindset: The New Psychology of Success* [DWE07], people realize that they can learn. People realize they are not just a product of their current talents and skills; they can learn at any time and get better. As a result, people can coach themselves into giving better results.

If managers and the people on the learning team know about the growth mindset, they can apply it to themselves. If managers have the growth mindset about their employees, they realize that they, the managers, have the job of creating an environment in which people can learn. That means that as soon as they have solo experts, the managers have to work to reduce the possibility of an indispensable employee.

13.5 Avoid the Scarcity Thinking Trap

If you think you only have one alternative—to maintain that indispensable employee where he or she is—reconsider. Indispensable people are a product of scarcity thinking. If you fall into the scarcity-thinking trap, you believe there are winners and losers, that you only have one alternative, that work is a zero-sum game. Don't believe it.

You have many alternatives to the idea of indispensable employees. What if that employee retired and went to Fiji to sip umbrella drinks? What would you do then?

Address the issue of your indispensable employees now, before they all do retire to Fiji or win the lottery. Prepare now.

13.6 Origins Of This Thinking

You might wonder how the software industry started to think this way. For decades, we've asked people to be heroic, to save the company by writing hundreds of lines of code overnight.

We didn't ask that the code be maintainable. We didn't ask for tests. We asked the hero to solve this problem *right now*!

We got what we asked for.

And we got something else: the notion of a "10X Developer" or an indispensable employee. Worse, senior managers often compensated those people with bonuses and other perks.

The industry fell for the hero mentality.

Heroes, experts, and "10X" people prevent everyone else from learning.

Even in the first edition of *The Psychology Of Computer Programming* [WEI11], Weinberg wrote about egoless programming: the idea that a team was stronger when its members worked together.

If you have indispensable people, ask them to create a better environment for everyone and more possibilities for their career track by working with teams, pairing with team members, offering to review or be a resource to a team, but not to be a hero.

Don't be surprised if you need to change your fellow managers' ideas about this trap. It's pervasive and threatens the ability of various teams to create the products you want and need.

13.7 Options to Stop Relying on Indispensable or 10X Employees

Your organization might be "addicted" to the fallacies of indispensable or 10X employees.

I offered some possibilities back in What Do You Do with Indispensable Employees? on page 127. Here are other possibilities you might consider to help the entire organization:

- Map the cycle time for either several weeks or for several features for any team with indispensable people. You will see bottlenecks in the flow of the work. You will see work queuing behind these people. You might even see fire drills or urgent work because they (unintentionally) block other people from doing that work. Now you have data.
- Stop rewarding heroics. Explain, "I want other people to learn this area of the code. I also want you to work a normal workweek. From now on, I will reward work where you bring other people into your expertise. I will not reward you for reinforcing the *same* expertise you have." You might need a longer conversation about the work people enjoy or prefer. This is probably not a one-time conversation, unless the person feels trapped by the work as I did.
- Make sure other people are available to work with the expert. Do not say you won't reward people and then not encourage other people to learn that area.
- This creates an environment where people can successfully stop reinforcing their current expertise. Now, consider these options:
- Never let experts work alone. Ask the team to monitor itself. Offer pairing or mobbing as possibilities whenever the expert would normally work alone.
- Ask the team to monitor its cycle time so everyone can see if they have wait states because of an expert.
- Reinforce the idea of flow efficiency, where the team works together, rather than resource efficiency.

I'll talk more about working as a team in Book 2.

CHAPTER 14
How Can I Do All of This Alone?

The most successful managers I've seen meet one-on-one with their managers regularly, often once a week.

Some other managers don't have enough access to their managers, so they use coaches for their one-on-ones. Some C-level managers use mastermind groups or executive roundtables. Those are small groups of people who help each other learn and obtain feedback and coaching from peers. Masterminds or these roundtables are not one-on-ones but might fulfill a similar purpose.

Managers need one-on-ones because unseasoned managers need feedback on how to make decisions, what the data might mean for future decisions, and when to act. That way, the manager learns how to delegate, how to coach, and how to see the data in the teams.

Even seasoned managers need to know the strategy, to understand if the company needs to pivot, and in general, reconnect to where the organization is headed.

See what happens when more senior managers don't conduct one-on-ones with the people they serve.

14.1 Myth: Good Managers Don't Need One-on-Ones

My company was in the midst of organizational chaos. We'd lost a huge contract with our largest customer. I was on my third VP of Engineering in the space of six months. And we had an opportunity to create a brand new product that would allow us to be first in our commercial space.

I was the Director of Software Engineering serving almost 100 people.

I made a one-on-one appointment with my new VP every week for six weeks. Every week he broke the appointment.

I sent him emails about certain decisions we needed to make. I rarely received an answer when I needed one. I got to the point where I explained two or three options and told him which option I would choose. He still didn't respond, so I made all the decisions.

He continued to break our one-on-one meeting appointments.

I was quite concerned. I decided after ten weeks of this non-communication that I would look for a new job.

I landed an offer in a week and decided to give my notice. I left my notice on his desk at 9 A.M.

At 9:22 A.M., he ran into my office, waving my notice. "You can't do this!" he yelled at me.

"Why not?" I asked.

"Because you're the only director getting anything done!" he yelled.

"How am I supposed to know that?" I asked. I'm pretty sure I didn't quite match his volume, but I was louder than normal. "Besides, that's not true. You've canceled every single one-on-one I booked with you. You can't possibly know what I'm doing and not doing and what my peers are doing and not doing."

He had no idea what we accomplished, our challenges, and where we needed help. Not as individuals and definitely not as a management team.

He was incongruent, blaming my colleagues for work he thought they didn't do. He attempted to placate me when he told me I was the "only" director finishing work. And he didn't see that the Engineering group needed his guidance to continue to set the context.

Everyone deserves a private time and place to speak with their manager. You can't and don't have to be a manager on your own. Your manager doesn't know what you're doing. And the more senior manager can't identify problems and fix the system of work. That system creates problems at your level and for the teams or groups.

14.2 Create Opportunities to See More of the System

Management one-on-ones allow the more senior manager to aggregate and see the larger system of work. I'll talk more about seeing your team's or group's system of work in Book 2.

Too many organizations tend to optimize for the individual or a team. Instead, the managers' roles are to optimize up at every opportunity. When managers meet with directors, and directors meet with VPs (and so on), the more senior manager can see bottlenecks and problems across the organization.

Not only can you address the system of work, managers require one-on-ones for feedback and coaching, especially about the individual people who present challenges to the less-seasoned manager.

14.3 Address Your Management Challenges

None of us is or can be perfect. You've seen several times in this book how one-on-one discussions with more senior and seasoned managers can support the less-seasoned manager. Those challenges must be private conversations. If you talk about people in public, others lose trust in you.

I hesitate to call these problems "people problems." Too often, someone—maybe even you—made a hiring mistake. You have someone who cannot find their way into the culture. Every organization manages these problems differently. Often, a person who doesn't fit in one group might fit in another. It's possible that person doesn't fit in the company at all. How do you make that decision and when? That's where your manager, often with the help of HR, can help.

Whatever you do, don't delay discussion of any of your management challenges. You will make decisions that aren't optimal. Instead of worrying about making the wrong decision, consider how you can make small, safe-to-fail decisions that you can change. See Wrong Decisions Happen on page 94.

14.4 Build Trust Both Ways

I didn't realize my manager trusted me to get the right work done. While I was glad of that, I didn't trust him. That's because we didn't have a working relationship.

He didn't serve my needs as a manager. He didn't support and serve me. I didn't need much, but I needed some support. I didn't get it.

How could I trust him?

We didn't have a relationship, never mind a trusting relationship.

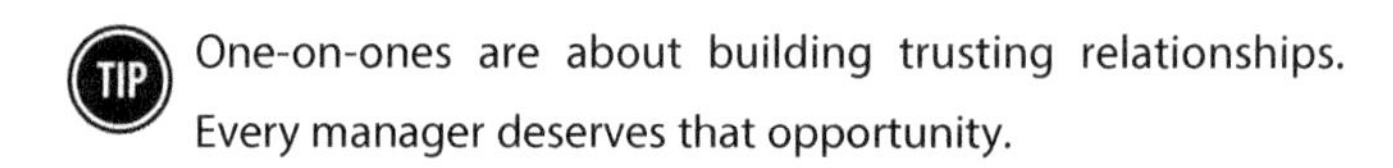

One-on-ones are about building trusting relationships. Every manager deserves that opportunity.

When managers meet on a regular basis in a one-on-one, they have the opportunity to build trust with each other.

14.5 Options to Create Regular One-on-Ones with Your Manager

When my VP and I finally spoke, he explained that he had been:

- Arranging for more funding for the company because we were still in startup mode.
- Talking the large customer into giving us another chance.
- Meeting with other customers to make sure we were never in this mode of getting more than 50% of our revenue from one customer again.

He was working as a CEO. He didn't realize he'd left the VP of Engineering position vacant.

Management is a balancing act. And I would have been fine if he'd told me. I would have understood the pressures he felt. I would have still needed some time with him on a regular basis.

Consider these options to create regular one-on-ones with your manager:

- Send an email outlining the two or three issues you want to discuss and the time you need. Don't feel you need to say the words "one-on-one."
- Ask if your manager is able to share some of the pressures. In this case, the manager might not feel as if he or she can delegate work. However, if you know of the pressures, you might be able to support your manager with other options.
- Explain the decisions you plan to make. You might offer options as I did and explain the options I planned to take as a default if he didn't answer. This is an example of stating intention, not asking for permission. See *Turn the Ship Around!* [MAR12] for more details.

I have also used the "ask for forgiveness later" approach. In that approach, I explained the problem and waited a short time for a decision. If the decision was later than what I needed, I acted in a way I thought worked for everyone. While that was mostly successful, I've had much better results now with intention.

There's one more option that might work for you. I've always wanted my one-on-ones during work hours. However, you might ask your manager to grab coffee earlier in the day or go out for dinner after work to discuss the issues. I'm not fond of this option because I want the work to occur in the workday. You might feel differently.

Managers need one-on-ones with their managers. You don't need to feel alone on your management journey.

CHAPTER 15

Where Will You Start Managing Yourself?

If you've read this far, you're curious and resourceful. Curious about what modern management is and resourceful for seeing and possibly already changing what you do.

I can't tell you where you should start because you're an expert on you, the people you serve, and your environment.

Remember, management is about creating an environment where people can do great work. What does your environment look like?

Here are some options that I've seen work in the past:

- Extricate yourself from being in the middle of other people's work.
- Admit mistakes as soon as you recognize you made them.
- Hone your feedback and coaching skills so you can help other people consider options where they don't depend on you for the answers.

Only you can decide where to start in your context. I recommend you first start with a self-assessment. Consider measuring your cycle time before you assess your behaviors.

15.1 Measure Your Cycle Time

Cycle time measures the time it takes to start and complete work. Typically, we think about cycle time for a team to deliver a particular outcome. I've found value in seeing my cycle time to see how much work I have in progress and where I have work and wait times.

As a manager, the longer you take to "deliver" a decision, clarify the outcomes, offer coaching or feedback, or perform any other management activity, the more you are an impediment *to* the team.

When I started to measure my cycle time, I created a positive feedback loop for myself. I limited my management WIP (Work in Progress). I made smaller decisions faster. That allowed me to consider more and smaller experiments.

Measure your cycle time with a value stream map similar to Figure 15.1, especially if you don't have too much parallel work.

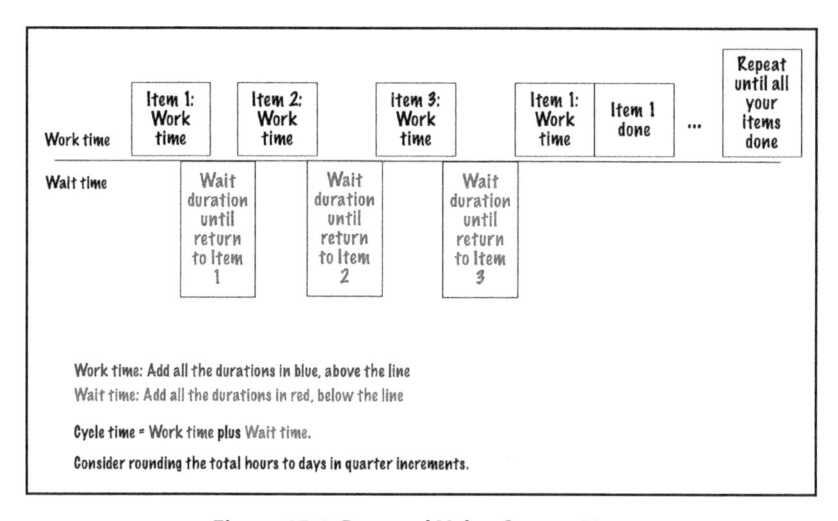

Figure 15.1: Personal Value Stream Map

To measure your cycle time, look for the work time: how much time does the item spend above the line? Now measure the wait time, or the length of time the item spends below the line. Add both of those times together to create your personal cycle time.

If you feel as if you're always past your ability to finish anything, consider this value stream map for each action item: See Figure 15.2 on page 139.

Here's how I drew that map for some managers:

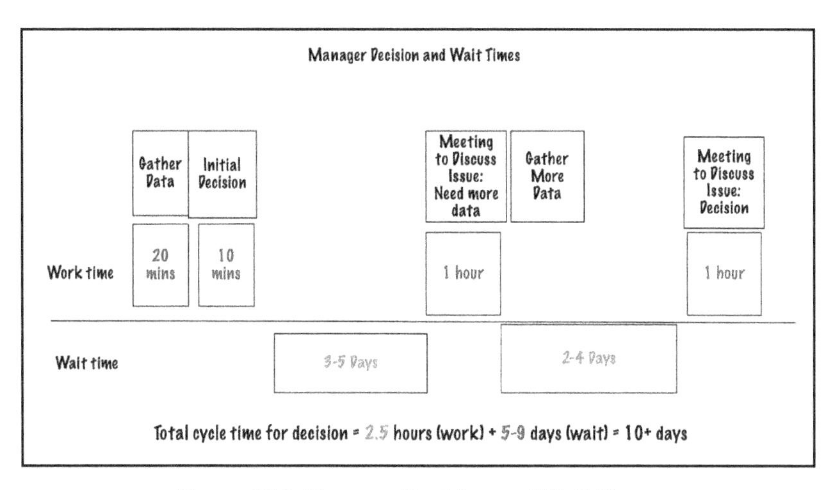

Figure 15.2: Manager Decision and Wait Times

1. Start with the very first state for the work item. That work starts above the line because you add value. In this case, you need to gather data.
2. Now, count the time the item stays in that work state. Keep the line in the value-add state, above the neutral line. Here, you make an initial decision.
3. Because the meeting to discuss that decision doesn't occur immediately, you now have a wait state. Show that delay below the neutral line. Here, the wait state is three to five days.
4. Once you start working on this item again, show the work above the neutral line. In that meeting, you now realize you need more data.
5. Show the delay to gather data below the neutral line. Here, the delay is two to four days.
6. You mark the work as done in the meeting that takes an hour to complete.

You might notice the wait time is a range of days. The managers could not remember exactly how long the various wait states took. Even taking their best guesses, each management decision took about

2.5 hours of work time, and at least five days of wait time, for a *minimum* cycle time of five-plus days.

Note that most of the time was wait time, not work time.

Dina, a manager, wanted to see how her many interruptions changed her cycle time, as in Figure 15.3.

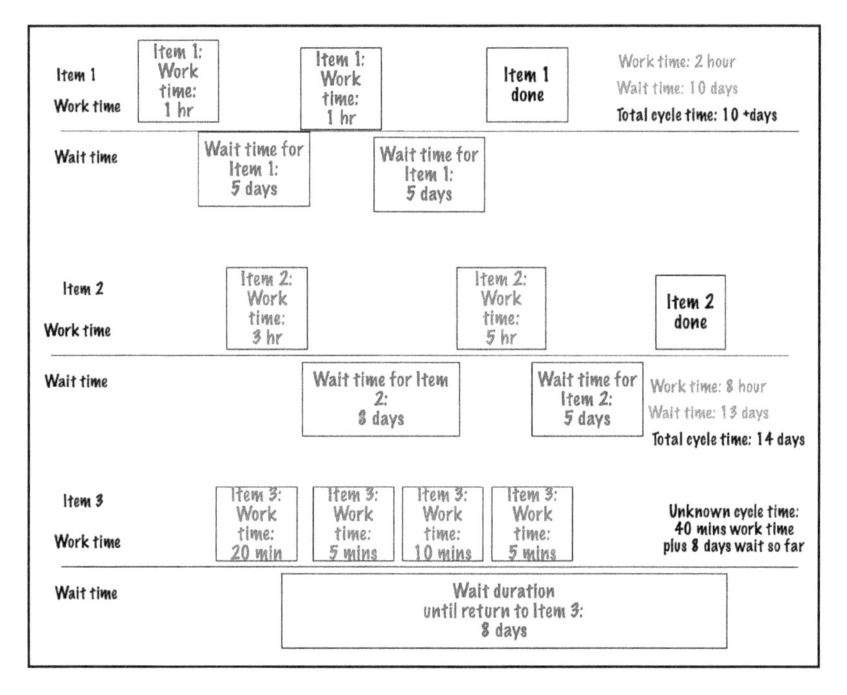

Figure 15.3: Parallel Personal Value Stream

Dina explained it in this way: "When I can get going on a specific action item, I can get it ready for the other people who need to discuss it with me. I still have to wait for them to be available because we don't act as a management team. However, when I can't spend enough time to *think* about the problem, as I did with Item 3, the work takes forever."

Dina used this value stream map to discuss what she did with her boss.

Managers often have to wait for other people, especially if the managers don't work as a team. Dina also had some technical work to complete. And she had deliverables to customers and to other teams across the organization.

These kinds of value stream maps help you see your interruptions and see where you create wait states for other people. You might want to deliver your items to the people you lead and serve *first*, so their work suffers from fewer delays.

Or, you might realize the work you deliver to others in the organization can speed your team's work.

Remember this: every interruption creates a wait state for some other work—yours or your team's. (See Book 3 for more details about cycle time for management teams.)

Now, you can assess your behaviors to see if you want to change your cycle time.

15.2 Assess Your Behavior Now

Here are some ways to gather data about your current behavior.

1. Look at this week and maybe next week's worth of meetings on your calendar. In how many of those meetings are you in the middle of the problem definition and the problem-solving? You might not be delegating enough.
2. How often do you need to ask for status? Is it the majority of the meetings? You might be micromanaging.
3. Consider recording yourself to see how you talk with people at meetings. Do you treat people as if they are equals? If not, you might think you're more valuable than other people.
4. Do you have indispensable employees? Up until now, have you encouraged people to be indispensable? You might have reinforced bottlenecks and lack of empowerment in other people.

Also, consider the options in each chapter to start changing your behaviors.

15.3 Change Behaviors Before Beliefs

Every time I wanted to make a change in my life, I changed my behaviors before I changed my attitude, values, and beliefs. For me, changing my behaviors was key to permanent change.

If you want to change any of your current beliefs, consider creating and practicing experiments. That's a great way to change your behaviors. What kinds of experiments can you create for the changes you want to make? You might consider these ideas:

1. Conduct a one-on-one with every person you serve at least biweekly for 20 minutes.
2. Only collaborate—not take work yourself—with technical people on technical work, such as pairing or mobbing.
3. Encourage people to estimate their own work.
4. Encourage people to explore problems themselves. Offer help in the form of thinking about the problem. Even if you're nervous about their solutions, remember your role is to support their problem-solving as much as possible. Review the ideas in How Much Do You Trust the People You Serve? on page 115 for ideas about where to start.
5. Encourage people to bring you problems when the problems are small.

See how you can become more congruent. No blaming, placating, super-reasonable, or irrelevant behaviors.

You might consider a checklist for your actions as you think about what you want to change. When I decided to change my management activities, I used these ideas for my checklist:

- Wait for the other person to talk before I decide I know the solution. That waiting helped me build better relationships.

- How much more can I delegate? What other information would I need to be more comfortable delegating?
- How can I help this person see and solve problems without solving the problem for them?

These questions helped me create a checklist for my behaviors. You might need different questions to address your behaviors.

15.4 Why Do People Not Know About These Ideas?

Maybe as you read these essays, you thought, "Well, this makes sense. Why didn't I know about this before?"

Most of what people "know" about management arises from popular books and accounting, not from the study of management.

Let's take a short journey through the history of management.

Up until the Industrial Revolution, people had very few choices if they wanted to eat and have a home: they handcrafted their products or worked in agriculture, often on the family farm. Some people worked in the arts.

That meant most people worked alone or in very small teams. These teams were small collaborative ventures.

You might call these "closely-held" entities. They weren't corporations as we know them now. They were more or less collaborative.

People didn't need much direct supervision or management. They needed to know where they were headed and the specific responsibilities they had. Because they could see each other or they reconnected each day, they didn't need a lot of direction. By the time they were adults, they knew how to work.

Two things changed how people worked. The first was slavery, and the second was the Industrial Revolution.

During slavery, people with money built large agricultural enterprises—often with hundreds of enslaved workers doing the manual labor.

In the Industrial Revolution, people with money built factories. They offered more pay to work in these factories than people could make on a farm or in the arts.

In both slavery and factory work, people needed to know what their jobs were. Often, the jobs or the inventory needed to be sequenced. That sequencing gave rise to Taylor's *Scientific Management.*

If you look at the balance sheets from the plantations—yes, those that used slave labor—they look eerily similar to current balance sheets. Too many contemporary "management" still accounts for people as if they were property to be bought and sold—resources to use and nothing more.

Much of our contemporary management beliefs and actions arise from slavery. (See *Accounting for Slavery: Masters and Management* [ROS18] for details.) Yes, that includes cost accounting.

I was horrified when I read that.

It's time for new thinking and new actions.

15.5 You Don't Have to Be Perfect

Remember the goal of managing yourself: to build effective relationships with your team members and across the organization. These relationships will help you accomplish more.

You cannot do "it" all yourself, regardless of what "it" is.

You don't have to be perfect at managing yourself. I have found it worthwhile to periodically examine my beliefs and actions to see if what I do helps or hurts my management.

I recommend you do the same.

You are human, so you can't be perfect. The people you serve need to see that you're trying and learning every day. They will then extend you the trust that you need to be a great manager.

Build your congruent behaviors, so you respect yourself first. Build your self-esteem. That will help you bring integrity to your work.

I hope you join me in Book 2 about leading and serving—managing—others.

Annotated Bibliography

[AVE16] Avery, Christopher. *The Responsibility Process.* Partnerwerks, Pflugerville, TX. 2016. Several fine discussions about responsibility and accountability; leading yourself first, and sharing leadership.

[BER14] Berger, Warren. *A More Beautiful Question: The Power of Inquiry to Spark Breakthrough Ideas.* Bloomsbury, New York, 2014. In our organizations and in our lives, we don't ask this question often enough: "Why are we doing this particular thing in this way?" This book explains why and helps us see alternatives.

[BRO12] Brown, Brené C. *Daring Greatly: How the Courage to Be Vulnerable Transforms the Way We Live, Love, Parent, and Lead.* Penguin Group, New York. 2012. Managers need courage to manage themselves. You can't be authentic without courage and vulnerability. And, you can improve your self-esteem when are authentic and congruent.

[BRO10] Brown, Brené C. *The Gifts of Imperfection: Let Go of Who You Think You're Suppose to Be and Embrace Who You Are.* Hazelden Publishing. 2010. None of us is perfect. We can try and still fail. This book helps us regain our self-esteem and authenticity when we "fail."

[DEC71] Deci, Edward. "Effects of Externally Mediated Rewards on Intrinsic Motivation" in *Journal of Personality and Social Psychology*

Vol 18, No 1. Also available at https://selfdeterminationtheory.org/SDT/documents/1971_Deci.pdf. A quote from the conclusion: "Money may work to"buy off" one's intrinsic motivation for an activity. And this decreased motivation appears . . . to be more than just a temporary phenomenon."

[DWE07] Dweck, Carol. *Mindset: The New Psychology of Success.* Ballantine Books, New York, 2007. This book discusses the fixed mindset and the growth mindset. If you have the fixed mindset, you believe you can only do what you were born with. If you have the growth mindset, you believe you can acquire new skills and learn. The growth mindset allows you to improve, a little at a time.

[GRE02] Greenleaf, Robert K. *Servant Leadership: A Journey into the Nature of Legitimate Power and Greatness, 25th Anniversary Edition.* Paulist Press, New York, 2002. The original and definitive text on servant leadership. The forewords and afterwords provide significant value to understanding how servant leaders work.

[KEI08] Keith, Kent M. *The Case for Servant Leadership.* Greenleaf Center for Servant Leadership, Westfield, IN, 2008. Useful because it's short, sweet, and specific.

[MAR12] Marquet, L. David. *Turn the Ship Around!* Penguin, New York. 2012. A fascinating perspective on how changing how we speak can change how we work. When we explain our intention, we don't have to ask for permission, before or after the fact.

[MCW96] McLendon, Jean and Gerald M. Weinberg. "Beyond Blaming: Congruence in Large System Development Projects" (1996) in _PSL Reader_ by Esther Derby, Don Gray, Johanna Rothman, and Gerald M. Weinberg. This specific article discusses how a culture of blaming often arises from the very top of the organization.

[PEL08] Pellegrini, Ekin K. and Terri A. Scandura. "Paternalistic Leadership: A Review and Agenda for Future Research" in *Journal of Management,* 2008. Retrieved at http://citeseerx.ist.psu.edu/

viewdoc/download?doi=10.1.1.475.7385&rep=rep1&type=pdf. It's possible that paternalistic management may well serve people in Eastern cultures. However, paternalistic management does not often serve people in Western cultures well.

[PIN11] Pink, Dan. *Drive: The Surprising Truth About What Motivates Us.* Riverhead Books. 2011. All motivation is intrinsic: autonomy, mastery, and purpose. Once people believe they are paid fairly, it's all about autonomy, mastery, and purpose.

[BCD05] Rothman, Johanna and Esther Derby. *Behind Closed Doors: Secrets of Great Management.* Pragmatic Bookshelf, Dallas, TX and Raleigh, NC, 2005. We describe the Rule of Three and many other management approaches and techniques in here.

[ROT12] Rothman, Johanna. *Hiring Geeks That Fit.* Practical Ink, 2012. Learn to hire people, from writing a job description to a great first day. All the templates are available for free on Johanna's website. The book explains how to use them.

[ROT17] Rothman, Johanna. *Create Your Successful Agile Project: Collaborate, Measure, Estimate, Deliver.* You don't need to adopt a specific framework for any given agile project. Instead, use the agile and lean principles to adjust for your project's context.

[RE14] Rothman, Johanna and Jutta Eckstein. *Diving for Hidden Treasures: Uncovering the Cost of Delay in Your Project Portfolio.* Practical Ink, 2014. A book about Cost of Delay and how to see how those costs affect your project portfolio.

[ROS18] Rosenthal, Caitlin. *Accounting for Slavery: Masters and Management.* Harvard University Press. 2018. The origins of our accounting and management practices arise from the practices of slave-owners back in the 1700s and 1800s. I didn't weep. I became angry. You might, too.

[SIN09] Sinek, Simon. *Start with Why: How Great Leaders Inspire Everyone to Take Action.* Penguin, New York. 2009. At the start of the book, he says that everything starts with "a decision." When leaders choose to start with why (his golden circle) they inspire. Everyone becomes more than they dreamed they were capable of being.

[SUT07] Sutton, Robert. I, PhD. *The No Asshole Rule: Building a Civilized Workplace and Surviving One That Isn't.* Illuminating exposé of why bullies and other assholes create a damaging workplace.

[TAL12] Taleb, Nassim Nicholas. *Antifragile: Things That Gain from Disorder.* Random House Publishing Group. 2012. The core idea is the more resilient we can make our organizations (and ourselves), the less fragile we are. It's not an easy book to read. However, the larger our span of influence, the more we need antifragility.

[WEI11] Weinberg, Gerald M. *The Psychology of Computer Programming: Silver Anniversary eBook edition.* Weinberg and Weinberg, 2011. I read the original (1971 edition) book just before I graduated with my Computer Science degree. I'd come off a disastrous "team" project. I read the part about egoless programming and decided to continue with software as a career. If you haven't read either edition, do so. You won't regret it.

[WEI16] Weinberg, Gerald M. *Becoming a Technical Leader.* I read the original book back in the 1990s, and I learned just from reading it. Now, as I've practiced many of the ideas, I'm a better human and a better leader. The rule transformation practice is just one of the many gems in this book.

[WEI02] Weinberg, Gerald M. *More Secrets of Consulting: The Consultant's Toolkit.* Dorset House, New York, 2002. Consultants and managers have many actions in common. Most of all, they don't *do* much of the work. They facilitate and enable people work better. In this slim volume, Weinberg discusses Satir's self-esteem toolkit.

Every manager needs their yes/no medallion. If you only read that part, you might become a even more successful modern manager.

[WEI93] Weinberg, Gerald M. *Software Quality Management, Vol 2: First-Order Measurement.* Dorset House Publishing, New York, 1993. This particular Weinberg book has excellent definitions of congruence and human interaction.

More from Johanna

I consult, speak, and train about all aspects of managing product development. I provide frank advice for your tough problems—often with a little humor.

If you liked this book, you might also like the other books I've written: https://www.jrothman.com/books/:

Practical Ways to Manage Yourself: Modern Management Made Easy, Book 1

Practical Ways to Lead and Serve—Manage—Others: Modern Management Made Easy, Book 2

Practical Ways to Lead an Innovative Organization: Modern Management Made Easy, Book 3

Write a Conference Proposal the Conference Wants and Accepts

From Chaos to Successful Distributed Agile Teams: Collaborate to Deliver

Create Your Successful Agile Project: Collaborate, Measure, Estimate, Deliver

Manage Your Project Portfolio: Increase Your Capacity and Finish More Projects, 2nd ed

Agile and Lean Program Management: Scaling Collaboration Across the Organization

Diving for Hidden Treasures: Uncovering the Cost of Delay Your Project Portfolio

Predicting the Unpredictable: Pragmatic Approaches to Estimating Project Cost or Schedule

Project Portfolio Tips: Twelve Ideas for Focusing on the Work You Need to Start & Finish

Manage Your Job Search

Hiring Geeks That Fit

Manage It!: Your Guide to Modern, Pragmatic Project Management

Behind Closed Doors: Secrets of Great Management

In addition, I have essays in:

Readings for Problem-Solving Leadership

Center Enter Turn Sustain: Essays on Change Artistry

I'd like to stay in touch with you. If you don't already subscribe, please sign up for my email newsletter, the Pragmatic Manager, on my website https://www.jrothman.com. Please do invite me to connect with you on LinkedIn, or follow me on Twitter, @johannarothman.

I would love to know what you think of this book. If you write a review of it somewhere, please let me know. Thanks!

—Johanna

Index

M

V

CPSIA information can be obtained
at www.ICGtesting.com
Printed in the USA
BVHW042145140121
597921BV00015B/503